ELF WARFARE

Chris Pramas

First published in Great Britain in 2017 by Osprey Games (part of Osprey Publishing),
PO Box 883, Oxford, OX1 9PL, UK
1385 Broadway, 5th Floor, New York, NY 10018
E-mail: info@ospreypublishing.com

Osprey Publishing, part of Bloomsbury Publishing Plc

OSPREY and OSPREY GAMES are trademarks of Osprey Publishing, a division of Bloomsbury Publishing Plc.

A CIP catalogue record for this book is available from the British Library
Print ISBN: 978 1 4728 1056 4
PDF e-book ISBN: 978 1 4728 1057 1
EPUB e-book ISBN: 978 1 4728 1058 8
Page layout by: Emma-Louise Hellon
Typeset in Garamond, Gill Sans and 1786 GLC Fournier

Originated by PDQ Media, Bungay, UK
Printed in China by C&C Offset Printing Co., Ltd

17 18 19 20 21 10 9 8 7 6 5 4 3 2 1

www.ospreygames.co.uk

INTRODUCTION

Elves, like many common creatures in fantasy fiction, have their roots in our myths. They feature in stories that go back a couple of thousand years at least and are present to a greater or lesser degree in all the Germanic mythologies. While some such creatures maintain a fairly cohesive identity over time, elves have changed substantially through the ages. They may have been gods originally but if so, they were demoted from that lofty status. They were still magical beings though and were associated with beauty and sometimes sex (though rarely the fun kind). Sometimes they were called demons. Later elves became associated with the fae, and often conflated with various types of faerie. They also shrank alarmingly in this period, becoming tiny creatures in stories and songs. The Victorians gave elves pointed ears and stocking caps, and this led to the form most familiar to modern children: the Christmas elf. All the supernatural and sexual threats of previous elves were gone, replaced by tinkers who make toys for Santa Claus. In America elves were reduced even further to makers of sugary cookies.

Elves owe the restoration of their dignity to fantasy fiction. Starting with Lord Dunsany in 1924 in *The King of Elfland's Daughter*, things began to look up for elves. In *The Hobbit* and *The Lord of the Rings*, J.R.R. Tolkien brought them closer to their mythological roots but made them his own as well. Tolkien's elves were ultimately tragic, doomed by their own passions to ages of suffering before abandoning the world all together. With the monumental success of his work, Tolkien's interpretation was widely influential in the field of fantasy and beyond. Now elves – tiny no longer – inhabit hundreds of worlds in fiction and in games.

Elf Warfare is the third in the Osprey Adventures series that started with *Orc Warfare* and continued with *Dwarf Warfare*. The goal here is the same: provide a military and cultural analysis of a favorite fantasy race. You'll find concepts and themes that are familiar but some that are different as well. You can enjoy *Elf Warfare* as a work of fantasy in its own right, or a source of ideas for your roleplaying or miniatures game campaigns. The book is broken down into four chapters.

CHAPTER ONE: THE ELVES

This chapter introduces the elf race. It discusses their origins, gods, and magic, and the destructive war that tore the elf kindred apart. It then delves into the organization of the elven military and the arms and equipment it uses.

CHAPTER TWO: ELF TROOP TYPES

The five elven kindred field a great variety of troops, from core units like archers and spearmen to exotic units like tree runners and moon elf infiltrators. This chapter looks at each in turn, discussing its battlefield role and typical equipment.

CHAPTER THREE: ELF STRATEGIES AND TACTICS

Elves have been fighting from time immemorial and they have developed many stratagems. This chapter looks at the way that elves win wars. Battlefield tactics, naval tactics, and siege tactics are all looked at in turn.

CHAPTER FOUR: ELF VICTORIES

Finally Elf Warfare takes a detailed look at five famous victories of elven arms. There is one battle for each of the kindred, showcasing how the various types of elf have been able to win important victories. This chapter also provides some concrete examples of how the myriad of troop types were used in practice.

THE ELVES

Since the first sunrise, we have been here. We have lived in the forests and the glens, in the plains and in the mountains, on the sea and under the earth. We are the five kindred. Fire, earth, metal, wood, and water live in us. We are the elements and the seasons. We are nature's beauty and also its wrath. Stand with us and you will prosper. Stand against us and you will be destroyed.

Inscription, Great Temple of the Sun Queen

Elves are a proud and ancient race with a history that stretches back into the mists of time. Their chroniclers claim that elves were there at the world's first sunrise. Dragons might dispute that the elven race is quite that old. Scholars, however, are not rushing off to dragon lairs to ask them their opinion. Suffice to say that elves emerged well before the beginning of recorded history. And they should know – they were the ones who began recording it.

There are five kindred of elves, but they all share common physical characteristics. They are lithe and tall, with an average height of 6 feet. Elves are agile and dexterous, with excellent vision that can pierce the darkness and even better hearing. Their most famous physical characteristic is, of course, their pointed ears. They are a comely race that others often find hauntingly beautiful. Yet elves seem tinged with sadness. Perhaps it is because they live so much longer than other races. Elves live through more heartbreak and tragedy than any human ever could. They can live up to 300 years if their lives are not cut short by violence or calamity. It is a rare elf that lives a full lifespan, however, for the world around them is ugly and brutish. Elves do not always seek war, but too often it finds them.

THE ELVEN KINDRED

At the dawning of the elf race, it was divided into five great kindred. Each was associated with one of the five elements: earth, fire, metal, water, and wood. While each branch had its own strengths and weaknesses, the elves considered themselves to be one people. The Five Kindred settled different lands, but worked together to defeat common enemies. When they were united, the elves were unstoppable.

Alas, the golden age of the Five Kindred could not last. The earth elves got into squabbles with the other kindred. They felt their needs always came last, and their aid, while much desired, was seldom returned in kind. These growing resentments could have been addressed if the other kindred had taken them seriously, but they were busy pursuing their own agendas. Someone did notice, however, and this was to change elf history forever. The Abyssal Queen, a powerful demon, whispered in the ears of the earth elves. Slowly, she caused the cracks between the elf kindred to become chasms. She turned the earth elves away from their patron god, the Earth Queen, and soon there was war between the kindred.

The Kin-War was long and bitter. The earth elves were outnumbered, but the Abyssal Queen sent demon legions to fight with them. Finally, the loyal kindred defeated the earth elves and drove them deep beneath the surface. Since that time they have been known as the dark elves and they have become an evil and depraved race. The few earth elves who did not fall under the Abyssal Queen's spell became known as the moon elves, for reasons explained later in this chapter.

Today the elves are divided as follows:

Kindred	Common Name	God
Earth Elves (Traitor)	Dark Elves	Abyssal Queen
Earth Elves (Loyal)	Moon Elves	Moon Queen
Fire Elves	High Elves	Sun Queen
Metal Elves	Gold Elves	Sword Queen
Water Elves	Sea Elves	Storm King
Wood Elves	Green Elves	Horned King

Descriptions of gold elves, green elves, high elves, moon elves, and sea elves follow and it is these kindred that are the focus of *Elf Warfare*. Dark elves have taken another path entirely and are thus beyond the scope of this book.

GOLD ELVES

The gold elves are the crafters par excellence of the elven race. They have an affinity with metal that makes their weapons and armor prized by all the civilized peoples, except perhaps the dwarves (who are proud of their own craftsmanship). Originally known as the metal elves, no one calls them that anymore. For one thing, their goldsmithing is unparalleled. For another the sale of their jewelry, rings, and weaponry has made them fabulously wealthy. This has made the gold elves both secretive and cautious.

Once the gold elves lived in great cities like the high elves, but their wealth attracted armies, plunderers, and dragons. Now most remaining gold elf cities are well-hidden in mountain vales laced with glamours to deceive travelers. A few are entirely underground, but these are more difficult to keep hidden from the dark elves, who never pass up an opportunity to loot a gold elf city. The secretive nature of the gold elf cities makes trade with other elf kindred a slow process, as the first concern of the gold elves is always safety. This has made their creations

rarer still, which has only made them more valuable to the outside world.

Not all gold elves want to shut themselves away from the world, however. Rather than retreat to hidden cities, many gold elf clans settled in the lands of other elf kindred. In exchange for security and raw materials, these gold elf clans make weapons and armor for their kin and contribute troops towards the common defense. The clans are most likely to be found in the mighty high elf cities, but they settle among the other kindred as well. The work of expanding and fortifying green elf cavern cities is often undertaken by such clans, for example.

GREEN ELVES

The green elves, also known as the wood elves, are the masters of the great forests. They see themselves as the guardians and the protectors of the woodlands and the creatures that dwell therein. Those who despoil the forests – be they monsters, loggers, or invaders – are guaranteed to face the wrath of the green elves. While they generally keep to themselves and remain in their woodland strongholds, they sometimes send contingents to aid their elven kin. Their archers are particularly prized.

Green elves live in small settlements scattered throughout the forests. Their mages can make trees grow into nearly any shape, and this is how the green elves build their homesteads. Many are tree houses, which provide excellent protection against predators by being high off the ground. All wood elf dwellings are alive and growing. Dead wood and nails are no way to build in green elf lands.

Some green elf bands prefer a nomadic existence. They travel throughout the great forests, making camp and moving on as they please. These bands carry news and sometimes goods from settlement to settlement. Some wood elf cities also exist. Most of them are in natural cave complexes with good water sources that the elves have expanded over time. In times of great peril, many green elves come to these cavern cities to find sanctuary. Their beautiful and spacious galleries can hold many times the typical number of inhabitants, and they have deep stores as well as caverns dedicated to the production of food.

HIGH ELVES

The high elves are the largest and most dynamic of the elf kindred. They burn with an inner fire that drives them to try to master the world. The way they see it, they bring civilization, stability, and enlightenment to a dark and brutish reality. Their enemies would be quick to point out, however, that high elf armies also bring fire, death, and conquest.

The high elves, also known as the fire elves, live in great cities renowned for their strength and beauty. They are centers of learning, both mundane and magical, and also hubs of trade. Other races view these cities with envy and thus they must also be engines of war. So while there are gardens of staggering beauty and a flowering of the arts, there are also barracks and armories scattered throughout every city, and all adult elves must train routinely with spear and bow. There is also a professional army in every city that is always ready to protect its interests.

Of all the elf kindred, it is the high elves who have always been empire builders. They believe that there would be less war if the world was more civilized. Better that they conquer it than savages like the orcs or the endlessly squabbling humans. History has witnessed the spectacular rise and terrible fall of many high elf empires over the millennia. Oftentimes, high elves have ruled over lands encompassing others of their kin. It is not uncommon, for example, for wood elf forests and especially sea elf coastlines to become part of high elf empires. As long as the rulers respect the ways of life of the other kindred, these alliances can be powerful. When the imperious nature of high elves come to the fore that is when the trouble begins.

MOON ELVES

Once the earth elves were one people under the tutelage of their goddess, the Earth Queen. As described earlier in this chapter, a powerful demon known as the Abyssal Queen seduced and corrupted most of the earth elves. After a long and bitter war, these elves – now known as dark elves – were defeated and forced deep beneath the surface. The earth elves who had remained loyal had won a victory of sorts, but it was a hollow one. The Kin-War had decimated their people and the surviving loyalists were few. Worse still, the tragedy had changed the Earth Queen. Now she styled herself the Moon Queen. Once a goddess of birth and stability, she became a goddess of death and madness. Her children, unwilling to abandon her, became the moon elves. They retreated to hidden grottos and since then have maintained a secretive existence.

Even to the other elven kindred, the actions of the moon elves are bizarre. They disappear for decades at a time. They are rumored to practice strange rituals in the pools of their grottos. They often treat other elves with hostility. And yet, on more than one occasion, mysterious bands of moon elves have shown up on the eve of important battles, and fought with valor and sacrifice to ensure elven victory. Then they take their dead and disappear once again.

What the moon elves most desire is to return their goddess to sanity. Their leaders do not agree on how to bring this goal to fruition. Some believe that they must destroy the dark elves and wipe out the stain on their honor. Some think their fallen kin can be redeemed so the earth elves can be one people again. Others think the elven kindred as a whole must unite before the Earth Queen returns to them. The Moon Queen herself provides no answers. Her priests see visions in the grotto pools, but they are cryptic and touched by madness.

SEA ELVES

The sea elves, also known as the water elves, are the great adventurers of their race. They are mariners, explorers, and traders whose wanderlust is legendary. Not for them hiding from the world in forests and cities. Sea elves want to be on the deck of a fast ship with the wind at their back.

The coastline is, of course, where most sea elves dwell when not voyaging. There are pockets of water elves elsewhere, however. Some groups prefer to ply the rivers on great barges. Others settled in swamplands and use flat bottomed boats and skiffs to navigate the waterways. A few brave hidden underground rivers, but they must be forever wary of their dark elf kin.

The towns and smaller settlements of the water elves are perforce somewhat rustic. Many do the less glamorous but just as necessary job of fishing, seafood of course being a staple of their diet. Sea elves, while sometimes characterized as flighty by the high elves, are not bumpkins. There is much travel between their settlements and the far voyagers bring news, stories, and curiosities from all over.

Sea elves themselves are not great city builders, generally favoring to live in towns of a thousand or so elves scattered along their coastlines. Their traders know the value of cities, however, and readily establish themselves when welcomed. It is common, for example, to find sea elf quarters in high elf and even human cities on the coast. Here the trading houses establish themselves and make it their business to become indispensable to their home cities. In human cities they must walk a fine line, as too much success can make their competitors jealous. Human merchants have driven sea elves out of more than one city when they felt threatened.

ELF ARMIES

The host of all Kallarion readied itself for battle. From all over the empire the eagles had marched and now they united on the blasted plain for the final battle. The dark lord and his numberless minions awaited them. The elves steeled themselves on this day of days. They knew they must win a victory or face annihilation.

From the Chronicles of Kallarion

In ancient times the elves had no formalized military. They lived in scattered clans that were largely self-sufficient. In times of trouble, the able-bodied folk would gather under the chief and form what was called a clan-troop. These could vary in size between a dozen warriors to several hundred, depending on the size of the clan. Elven clans would sometimes join together to fight a common foe but these were temporary arrangements. Even today there are elves who live and fight in this fashion, most commonly wood elves and moon elves.

It was the high elves, with their dreams of empire, who advanced the military arts over the millennia. They created standing armies in their cities and organized them according to a common pattern, which then spread to other elven kindred. The elvish name for these armies translates to "glorious eagles of war and victory" but only the stuffiest academic text uses that terminology now. To soldiers, citizens, friends, and enemies, elven armies are known as eagles. Their structure varies somewhat by time and place, but typically an elf army is organized as follows:

- An eagle consists of at least two wings and is commanded by a general.
- A wing consists of three to ten talons and is commanded by a major.
- A talon consists of three to five troops and is commanded by a captain.
- A troop consists of twelve to twenty soldiers and is commanded by a sergeant.

As elves are small in number compared to their enemies, all adult elves who are able must spend time in military training. Typically, this is a three year period but in some places it is up to ten years. In those years the elves' primary job is that of a soldier, with training in melee and missile combat, maneuvering in formation, and battle tactics. Once this period of active service ends, they can go back to their civilian lives if they so choose. They remain on the rolls of their talon, however, and each summer they muster again for a few weeks to refresh their skills and meet and interact with the younger recruits. In this way the elves can call up nearly their entire adult population in times of war. Most crises are not so dire, so younger elves are called up first by year. When the aged veterans are called to serve, the situation must be truly desperate.

THE PROFESSIONALS

Some elves choose not to return to civilian life and become full time, professional soldiers. In times of peace their numbers are relatively small. Long service soldiers typically become sergeants or officers, though some become part of elite formations like the Star Knights. Major elven cities are home to military academies that train officers in strategy and tactics. Promising soldiers from all over vie to get into these prestigious schools. Military academies are typically a ten year commitment that mix classes with field training. Candidates graduate not just with a sound basis in theory but also with years of hands-on practice.

The wood elves and others without access to military academies use a mentorship system to train officers. Candidates are assigned as assistants to serving officers and learn on the job. The training is perforce less standardized but still can produce outstanding leaders. Typically under this system there is one mentor and one mentee. It's been found that this gives the best results, as the officer can concentrate on teaching the one candidate. If a war drags on, however, an officer may have to take on up to half-dozen mentees at once so the fallen can be replaced quickly.

ELF ARMOR AND WEAPONS

Elves are a long-lived race and their craftsmanship reflects this. While they can, when the need is acute, make things quickly, they prefer to take their time and make their crafts both functional and beautiful. This applies to weapons and armor just as much as it does to clothing and jewelry. Form matters as much as function, and sometimes even more so. A sword etched with a pattern of blooming flowers is cherished more than an unadorned blade, even if the latter cuts deeper.

As elves are generally tall and lithe, they prefer weapons that are lighter and quicker than many of their foes. They know that enemies like orcs and ogres are stronger than they are, so they rely on speed and skill to beat such opponents. Their weapons are designed to maximize the elves' natural gifts of agility and quickness. Similarly, armor is designed for the most protection with the least weight. None of this would be possible without the skill of elven smiths. They have spent millennia perfecting techniques that allow them to forge steel that is light but incredibly strong. This work is so beyond the skill of human smiths that they think the elves are working with a special metal not found in human lands. Stories of "faerie steel" are common, and elven smiths do little to dispel them. Their skills and techniques are the real treasure, so they'd rather have humans chasing a mythical metal than trying to learn their secrets.

Elves use a broad range of armor. Green elves, moon elves, and other light troops favor leather armor, as speed and stealth are integral to their tactics. Sea elves prefer it too, as heavier armor is a detriment when fighting on the water. High elves and other melee troops favor chainmail, as it provides a balance of weight and protection. Gold elves and certain elite units use plate armor, which offers unrivaled protection though at a high cost.

The most common melee weapons are spears and long swords. Spears are usually between 6 and 9 feet in length, though some units have been known to use weapons up to 12 feet long when facing cavalry heavy armies. Light troops favor short swords and sometimes hatchets. Battle axes are sometimes used but are much less common. Perhaps it is their long association with dwarves that puts elves off. Two-handed weapons like glaives and great swords are rarest of all, usually only used by elite formations like foot knights.

The weapon most associated with elves is, of course, the bow. Elf bowyers are just as skilled as the smiths and the elven longbow is truly a work of art. When used by properly trained archers (a process that takes many years), they shoot farther and hit harder than human or orc bows. The longbow is by far the most prevalent type of bow in use in elf eagles, but light cavalry and certain units like companions use the composite short bow instead. This cannot shoot as far as the longbow, but it handles more easily and still packs a punch.

The fletchers provide a variety of arrows for elf archers. The most common types are leaf arrows and branch arrows. Leaf arrows take their name from the broad shape of their arrowheads, and they are used in hunting and against lightly armored opponents in times of war. Even a glancing hit from a leaf arrow can cause a long cut that bleeds heavily. When facing more heavily armored foes, archers turn to branch arrows. These arrows have narrow heads with either a spike or a chisel point. The skill of elf smiths is once again on display with these arrowheads, as their points are hard enough to penetrate most armor. The spike variant works best against chainmail while the chisel variant is designed to punch through plate armor. Elf archers usually carry a mix of all these types of arrow.

Units of archers describe themselves as trunks from which sprout branch and leaf. Some elf units also use arrows for signaling. This is done using arrows that make whistling sounds. Different pitches indicate different orders. Even foes who understand that the elves are signaling each other don't have the ear for music that allows the elves to tell the subtle differences in pitch that indicate various commands.

ELF MAGIC

Elves are masters of magic. They have few rivals in this arena, for they have been studying magic for eons. That said, the path of the wizard is long and dangerous, and the number of powerful elf wizards is small. While the generals wish it were otherwise, it's a rarity that a wizard actually takes the field with an elven eagle. The nature of elven spellcraft is also a disappointment to war makers who want flashy and destructive magic on call. Wizards mostly use ritual magic, which can indeed be quite destructive, but rituals can take days and even months to complete. This is not helpful when a battle is going to be fought today. Ritual magic can have a powerful effect on military campaigns in the long term though. Elf wizards can summon up storms to lash enemy armies or bog them down in mud given the right circumstances. If the elves besiege a fortress or city, wizards could use earth magic to shake down its walls given time.

Elven magic is based on the five elements and the four seasons. It is a common misconception that each kindred can only use magic from its associated element. Many human scholars believe, for example, that high elves can only use fire magic and green elves can only use wood magic. In truth elves of one kindred have an aptitude for their element, but can learn magic of any element. Indeed, they must because elf magic is all about the complicated interplay of the elements and also the season. Certain rituals work better when cast in the appropriate season. A ritual to increase the fertility of land works best in spring, for example.

Elf magic comes into play in wartime most commonly in two ways: defensive enchantments and magic items. Defensive enchantments are effective because the rituals can be cast in times of peace, when time is an abundance resource. All but the youngest of elf cities, for example, have had their walls and towers fortified by earth magic. This makes them much more difficult to breach during a siege. Similarly, green elf forests are protected by a variety of enchantments to confuse and mislead invaders. Once enemies get inside an elven forest, they find it difficult to navigate and are easily lured into traps and ambushes. Elven ships are fast and durable because their planks are enchanted with water magic.

Magic items is a broad category that covers a variety of portable artifacts. Those most commonly seen on the battlefield are weapons and armor, and gold elves are the undisputed masters of this type of magic. Wizards of other kindred can and do use metal magic, but the gold elves' natural aptitude and millennia of practice make them the most skilled forgers and enchanters of magic weapons and armor. They can make weapons that can puncture plate armor with ease, and shields that can stand up to the mightiest blows. Some weapons burn with an inner heat or crackle with electricity. Others can freeze an opponent's limbs. Arrows are the most common magic item seen in elven eagles, as several can be enchanted at once. Most are simply better at penetrating armor. Some carry other effects, like bursting into flame on contact or causing wounds that won't heal naturally.

For themselves wizards make magic wands or staves. These they use for self-defense and to make direct attacks on the battlefield. Wands and staves take years to enchant and each has a limited number of magic effects. Some are always active. These are typically defensive, like an enchantment to protect the wizard from arrows and other missiles. Others can be used a certain number of times per day. Depending on the spell, its use may be limited to daylight or nighttime. The most destructive effects (lightning bolts, gouts of fire, etc.) can only be used once in a battle. A wizard with a powerful wand or stave can change the course of a battle, but the number of such wizards is small.

ELF TROOP TYPES

Elven armies are quite varied, as each of the kindred fights in its own way. Some troop types are common among all the kindred and others are unique to one or two. This chapter breaks down the various elements of elven eagles and looks at each in detail. Enemy generals who think that every elven army is the same are in for a surprise.

ARCHERS

We outnumbered the elf army but many of our infantry units were made up of ill-trained conscripts with little in the way of training or armor. I told the general a frontal attack was suicide. He called me a coward and led the charge in person. It is a mercy he was killed in the first volley. He never had to see the army break and run or the piles of arrow riddled corpses.

Nasreen, Human Commander of Horse

Archers are the heart of the elven military tradition. Simply put, there are no better units of missile troops than elven archers. Some say that elves are just natural marksmen, but there is more to it than that. It is true that elves are dexterous by nature, with excellent hand/eye coordination. Equipment and training are just as important, however. Elves long ago mastered the arts of bowyer and fletcher. The elven longbow is a powerful weapon but all but useless to those without proper training. Thus elves of all kindred start at a young age and that training never ceases. Even the oldest elves still come out to archery butts a couple of times a week. Younger elves shoot every day. Clans, towns, and cities have regular competitions to encourage the pursuit of marksmanship.

In times of war up to half of an elven force may consist of archers. In some case the percentage is even higher. They are deployed and used in different ways, depending on the situation and the kindred involved. Green elf archers usually fight as skirmishers, which makes sense for forest terrain. High and gold elf archers can use skirmish tactics, but also form up into large units that can unleash devastating volleys. Sea elf training focuses on naval combat. Their role is to sweep enemy decks of their crew with accurate fire. Due to their small numbers, moon elves most often take on the role of snipers. They target leaders and standard bearers, with the aim of undermining the enemy's morale.

Archers are usually lightly armored, with leather jerkins or perhaps chainmail shirts. They carry short swords or dirks for close defense, and while quite adept with those weapons they can't stand for long against enemy shock troops. An elven archer generally goes into battle with at least 40 arrows and keeping them supplied is an important part of any battle plan. Their rate of fire is such that they can loose all their arrows in a matter of minutes. Support troops must be ready with fresh arrows or the archers will become a spent force in short order.

SPEARMEN

The wagons with the wounded need time to get to safety. We plant our spears here and we will not be moved!

Melidel, Elf Captain

Spearman are the most common melee troops in elven armies. They fight in close formation, creating a thicket of spear points that can repel both cavalry and infantry formations. Most such units wear chainmail and carry shields they can interlock for increased defense. They carry short swords as secondary weapons, which can be quite handy when enemies get beyond units' spear points.

High elves deploy their spearmen in large phalanxes that are difficult to shift. These units are up to ten ranks deep, and when they push forward they are hard to resist. Gold elves developed an even heavier type of unit that eschewed shields so they could wield longer and longer spears. These days such troops wear plate armor for protection and use both hands to handle pikes that are up to 16 feet long.

Green elves, though identified strongly with hit and run missile tactics, do maintain units of spearmen, though they use them differently than their kindred. They can and do form shield walls, especially when they want to block choke points in the forest. Green elf spearmen can form up and tear down a shield wall in a matter of seconds, though they are typically only three or four ranks deep. They are not designed to get into long slogging matches with enemy troops, however. They are meant to have short, sharp engagements while other green elf troops perform flanking maneuvers and bring more archers to bear.

SWORDSMEN

Arrows killed my horse so I found myself on foot once again. I had just gathered a few of my men when elf swordsmen slammed into our flank. I thought I was a fair bladesman but they went through us in seconds and I was left for dead.

Thestor, Human Mercenary Sergeant

While archers and spearmen are the dominant types of elven infantry, units of swordsmen also appear in the order of battle. They provide eagles with a solid medium infantry that is able to attack or defend as tactics require. Swordsmen typically wear full chainmail armor and carry large shields. They wield long swords designed for slashing and thrusting as the situation merits. These "sword and board" troops can hold their own against most enemy infantry once they are formed up. Typically, units of swordsmen are deployed behind spearmen and are used to shore up the battle line or counter-attack once the enemy has lost its impetus. They are skilled fighters, many of whom have spent decades learning the finer points of bladework.

High elves field swordsmen most frequently and often use them as garrison troops. Gold elves prefer heavy infantry but do field swordsmen to fill out their ranks. Green, moon, and sea elves prefer their swordsmen to be less encumbered, so they wear chain shirts only and carry smaller shields. This makes them more mobile, which suits the fighting style of those kindred better.

FOOT KNIGHTS

Two of the knights with glaives used their weapons to trip the rampaging troll. It only fell to its knees but that was enough. My two-handed sword crunched into its neck. The troll looked at me stupidly, as its blood gushed all over. Then it fell on its face and expired.

Selwyn, Knight of the Chalice

The heaviest infantry in an elven eagle are the foot knights. They are elite formations made up of highly trained warriors in full plate armor and wielding two-handed weapons such as halberds, glaives, and great swords. Gold elves and high elves maintain knightly orders to recruit and train these feared shock troops. The most famous of these orders are the gold elves' Knights of the Chalice and the high elves' Knights of the Phoenix. Entry into these orders is based on merit only. Family bloodlines are not considered. Candidates must be experienced warriors with proven skill, strength, and endurance. Foot knights must face the toughest opponents on the battlefield and they must be ready for them.

The foot knights have a friendly rivalry with their mounted brethren such as the Star Knights and Griffon Knights. They consider the mounted knights to be glory hounds who want to win the battle with one charge. The foot knights pride themselves on their ability to get into extended slogging matches with the fiercest enemies and come out victorious. When trolls or orc Ironbacks are rampaging though the battleline, it is the foot knights who are called upon to stop them. Only they have the armor, weapons, and expertise to deal with enemy shock troops.

As they are elite troops and expensive to maintain, the number of foot knights is never large. A typical elven eagle might have one unit of foot knights and they must be used judiciously. They often act as a bodyguard to the general until the moment of decision arrives. Then they are committed where the danger is the greatest. Some generals like to lead them personally into the fray. While this is an honor, most foot knights prefer it if the general stays backs and concentrates on commanding the eagle. Only the rarest of generals has the skill to keep up with the foot knights and they'd rather focus on defeating the enemy than protecting a leader who is not well-versed in their fighting style.

COMPANIONS

We tore into the elf line, hammering down on their shields and driving them back. We pushed them and pushed them but suddenly the line firmed up and orcs were falling all around me. I turned around to wave the boys forward but there was no one left behind me. Sneaky elves with puny bows had shot them all down.

Torgar, Orc Warchief

Companions are specially trained and equipped archers pioneered by gold elves but sometimes used by other kindred as well. Unlike regular archers, they use composite short bows instead of longbows and wear full chainmail. Their role on the battlefield is to provide close support to melee troops. Companions must be able to fight in formation or in skirmish order, shoot accurately while the melee swirls close by, and know when to engage and when to break off. This requires discipline, good judgment, and a great deal of training.

A unit of companions forms immediately behind a melee unit such as spearmen, swordsmen, or foot knights. Typically, these two units train together, as they must fight in unison on the battlefield. Companions let other archer units shoot at long range and begin the reduction of enemy numbers. As enemy melee troops approach, companions began to shoot volleys of arrows. When this is no longer practical, they break into a skirmish formation and take up position on either side of the unit they have been paired with. In the ensuing melee, they move around the flanks of the enemy unit if possible and shoot at it at point blank range. Here the power of the composite bow comes into its own and companions shoot the enemy down at ranges closer than any other archers would dare. If they cannot flank the enemy, they shoot over the heads of their allies into the rear ranks of the enemy.

Companions carry short swords and when necessary, they can get stuck into a melee but this is a last resort. They provide better support with their bows. They are particularly lethal when enemy units break and run. Companions can continue shooting into the exposed backs of their foes long after the elf melee troops have stopped their pursuit.

SCOUTS

The scouts report that the dwarves have split their war host in two. One part is heading for the bridge and the other the ford upstream. This is the chance we've been waiting for. We can concentrate our wings on one of these forces

Scouts are the eyes and ears of an elven army. They are recruited out of the archers and each one is an expert shot and tracker. They are also masters of stealth and camouflage, and can move unnoticed in most terrain. Their primary job is not to attack, but to monitor enemy movements and make sure elven commanders have a clear picture of what is happening on the battlefield. They communicate this information through coded signals or runners. The signals sound like bird calls to the untrained ear but scouts can transit sophisticated information using this method. For particularly important messages, they will send a runner back to headquarters. Since scouts usually operate in troops of a dozen or so, the number of runners available is perforce limited.

Scouts can and do fight when necessary. Most frequently, they clash with their opposite number. If they detect enemy scouts in the field, they attempt to mislead them or ambush them if this proves impossible. Denying the enemy's leadership information is an important task. Scouts sometimes attack isolated enemy units to sow confusion in their ranks as well.

Elven scouts carry bows and short swords, and sometimes hatchets as well. The latter are useful for woodcraft and can also be used in hand to hand combat. A few scouts wear leather armor but most wear no armor at all. They need to be able to move quickly and silently and most don't want the weight of even leather armor when they are on a mission. This is another reason the quick strike from ambush is their preferred tactic. They are not cut out for a drawn out fight. If things go wrong, scouts melt back into cover and make their way back to elven lines.

TREE RUNNERS

That forest was a death trap. Dealing with the elves shooting at you from behind every tree was bad enough, but arrows also rained down on us from archers up in the trees! Tricky buggers never came down to fight us with honor, just ran through the branches and pelted us with missiles. I've never seen so many head wounds in all my years of campaigning.

Valan, Human Soldier

Among the green elves there is a cadre of skirmishers who specialize in three-dimensional warfare. While all wood elves are skilled climbers, the tree runners are capable of amazing acrobatic feats. They can move quickly in the treetops, jumping from bough to bough. In the dense forests of the great green elf homelands, they can make lengthy journeys without their feet touching the ground.

Due to their stealth and agility, tree runners excel at ambush tactics. Most commonly, they will position themselves above and behind an enemy unit and then unleash volleys of arrows upon them. In dark and tangled forests, it is not immediately obvious where the attack is coming from and this only adds to the confusion. Some tree runners like to get right over a unit and throw javelins or drop rocks on enemies instead. Caches of these weapons, as well as extra arrows, are prepared beforehand and hidden up in trees in likely avenues of approach.

Tree runners with time to plan also prepare traps in their chosen ambush sites. They may seed the ground with caltrops to hamper enemy movement. They may use rope to suspend heavy stones or dead wood from tree branches, ready to drop these on unsuspecting enemies. They've even been known to locate beehives before an engagement, so they can be thrown into enemy units. The hive itself does little damage but the angry bees that burst forth can create chaos in disordered enemy units. If faced with a weight of return missile fire, tree runners disappear into the treetops and redeploy somewhere else. They are a devilish nuisance to enemy commanders, who have been known to resort to lighting fires to smoke them out of the trees. Starting a fire in the middle of the forest your army occupies is, of course, not always the best idea…

MOON ELF INFILTRATORS

The general's tent was like an abattoir. So much blood. He and all his bodyguards were dead. And though there were troops not ten yards away, no one had heard a thing. No clang of weapons. No death screams. Nothing.

Stoddard, Priest of the Emerald Order

Moon elves are the smallest kindred by far. They do maintain units of traditional elven troop types, but they have had to learn to make war in other ways. The infiltrators typify this style of fighting. They are small teams of two to twelve soldiers who specialize in irregular warfare. They use ambush and hit and run tactics to cause confusion behind enemy lines. They are masters of night fighting, using stealth techniques and their elven vision to turn darkness into a time of terror for the foe. They have also been known to perform decapitation strikes against enemy leadership. Sometimes they will conceal themselves on a battlefield the night before an expected battle, only revealing themselves when they

have a chance to kill important leaders like generals or spell casters. This has changed the course of several important battles. However, the moon elves make their own plans and do not share them with their allies, which sometimes leads to tension. Their operations sometimes wrong foot their allies, but the moon elves as always pursue their own goals.

Since infiltrators rely on stealth, they are generally lightly armed and armored. In most engagements they wear leather armor and carry compact weapons like short swords, hand crossbows, daggers, and short bows. Some have mastered unusual weapons like whips and crescent staves. The latter are short staves with a blade in the shape of a crescent moon. An infiltrator typically fights with one in each hand, but they can also be snapped together to form a longer weapon with a blade on each end. This is done when the fighting gets hot and survival becomes more important than stealth.

MARINES

The seaward wall was all but undefended in the siege. It was impossible to land troops there, or so we thought. Damn sea elves swam over the reef and then scaled the walls while we slept. We woke the next morning to find the gates of the city open and elf marines in the towers drinking our booze.

Randulick, Guard of the Tragano Garrison

Elven warships have contingents of specially trained soldiers, the vast majority of whom are sea elves. The job of the marines is not to sail the ship (that's what the sailors do) but to fight. They specialize in boarding actions, and are well-versed in offensive and defensive tactics in ship combat. When their ship closes with an enemy vessel, it is the marines who swarm over the gap to seize it.

At sea the marines do not usually fight in formation. Boarding actions are much more chaotic affairs, so they fight in loose groups at best. As both hands are often needed for balance, few marines use shields. Heavy armor is also not prudent when at sea, so leather jacks and chain shirts are about the only armor used and even they are rare. Armament is very much an individual choice to a marine. They are generally armed with some combination of cutlasses, rapiers, hand axes, maces, and boarding pikes. About a quarter of the marines also have bows. They tend to stay on their own vessel and provide support for the attackers, or defend the ship if it is being boarded. Full units of sea elf archers are also sometimes assigned to a ship, particularly if a naval battle is expected.

While marines' primary role is shipboard combat, they do sometimes fight on land. They may be landed to attack a fort or a town. In dire circumstances, the navy sends a unit of marines to reinforce the eagles. The marines don't particularly care for this kind of combat. Their training is not in formed units and shoulder to shoulder fighting. Still, the marines have their uses in a land battle. They can be fielded as light infantry, dealing with enemy skirmishers, raiding baggage trains, and the like. They have, on occasion, served as garrison troops, but generals prefer other troops for such duty. Leaving marines in the proximity of so many taverns is an invitation to indiscipline.

BEAST HANDLERS

The elves are always on about how much more civilized they are than us. Tell that to my soldiers who were ripped apart by wild dogs!

Sergeant Minyas, The Azure Company

In ancient times elves of all the kindred used animals in battle. Today it is primarily the green elves who carry on that tradition. Every community includes expert beast handlers. Some of them take care of horses and others domestic animals, but a specialized core of handlers train animals for war.

The favored animal for this is the so-called elven woodhound, a tough breed of dog that excels at hunting and takes easily to battle training. Woodhounds are fast and pugnacious. They can bowl over an infantryman

or drag lightly armored cavalry from the back of their mounts. Some woodhounds are even fitted with hardened leather armor for protection, which is often spiked to make them difficult to grapple with. Other animals sometimes trained by beast handlers include the kellinor (a big cat similar to a puma), hawks, and even bears on occasion.

Various other birds are also used for communication purposes. The moon elves don't use animals to fight, but they do use owls to carry messages between their communities.

In times of war the beast handlers choose their animals and guide them carefully to the field of battle. The handlers themselves wear little armor so they can keep up a good pace. They are typically armed with a bundle of javelins and a short sword. They fight if necessary but their job is to direct the animals and to control them as much as possible. They are also trained in husbandry and can treat their animals' wounds after the battle is over.

LIGHT CAVALRY

Dwarf ballistas are deploying on the right flank. We must ride down their crews before they get those machines set up and shooting. Follow me, sabers at the ready. Speed of horse!

Telewyn, Elf Captain

Elven armies maintain various units of light cavalry for reconnaissance, communication, and pursuit. The green elves have their Forest Riders, the high elves their Border Rangers, the sea elves their Coast Watchers, the gold elves their Steel Wardens, and the moon elves their Night Stalkers. All of these units share common equipment and tactics. Light cavalry are usually armed with composite short bows and curved sabers ideal for passing slashing attacks. Some also carry spears or javelins. They wear either leather armor or chainmail.

The main responsibility of the light cavalry is finding the enemy and keeping track of their movements. On their swift elven steeds, they are difficult to catch and this lets them range far afield when scouting. Their speed makes it possible to provide timely intelligence to commanders on enemy dispositions. They also try to detect and neutralize enemy scouts.

Once battle is joined, light cavalry can take on many different roles. All are skilled horse archers, so they can speedily bring enemy units under fire and then ride away when threatened. Their sabers come out when dealing with enemy light troops, be they infantry or cavalry. When enemy units break and flee, the light cavalry ride them down swiftly.

HEAVY CAVALRY

The charge of the Griffon Knights was the most beautiful spectacle I have ever seen in a lifetime of campaigning. The glittering golden armor, the snapping pennants, the thundering horses – it was magnificent. I was so caught up in the moment I almost took a lance to the face.

Chellain, Paladin of the Pierced Heart

The heavy cavalry is the armored fist of an elven army. They are tall, strong elves on powerful steeds. High elves and gold elves are the kindred that make most use of heavy cavalry and it is their Star Knights and Griffon Knights respectively that are the most famous.

Heavy cavalry wear full plate armor and large shields, and are armed with lances, long swords, and maces, as befits their melee combat role. Their war horses too are armored with barding, which slows them down some but provides important protection. The cost in time and gold to train and outfit such troops is tremendous, so they are not committed to battle lightly. They simply cannot be replaced quickly so elven generals are always careful when deploying heavy cavalry.

Typically, the heavy cavalry are kept in reserve and committed when the battle swings in the balance. Their job is at once simple and difficult: break the enemy's main line of resistance. Most commonly this means crushing blocks of heavy infantry, though sometimes they face cavalry or even large creatures like ogres. Their most potent weapon is the charge. A line of elven knights thundering forward with lances leveled is nigh unstoppable. If they can impact and break the enemy with such a charge, it can end a battle. If the heavy cavalry gets bogged down in a lengthy melee, that's when it becomes vulnerable.

DRAGOONS

The day we captured General D'Bruzza was truly glorious. He had ridden ahead of his army with a light escort to the frontier fort he planned to use as his headquarters in the coming campaign. We left the front gate open and he rode right in. Imagine his surprise to find the fort already occupied by several hundred dragoons!

Neniel, Elf Dragoon

Dragoons are mounted infantry troops. Unlike cavalry, they are not trained or equipped to fight on horseback. Rather they use horses for transport but dismount to fight. Dragoons were pioneered, strangely enough, by the sea elves. When they raided from their ships, sea elf sailors and marines would seize all the horses and mules they could find and use them to cover ground more quickly. Infantrymen grumbled that this was because seamen couldn't handle a day of real marching, but military leaders realized the idea had merit. Soon other kindred were experimenting with mounted infantry and now they are a regular feature of gold elf and high elf armies. Moon elves also took the concept. It allows them to deploy speedily, but then dismount and use the stealth tactics they are famous for. The name dragoon is derived from a now famous incident in which a high elf knight asked a sea elf on a stolen mule what he was supposed to be. "A dragon of the sea!" the soldier replied proudly. The sea elf's low brow accent confused the knight, who asked, "What on earth is a dragoon?" The story spread and the name stuck.

Most dragoons are armed and equipped as swordsmen, spearmen, or companions. About a quarter of their number are archers. They are used when it's imperative to get infantry to a strategic point as soon as possible. They frequently join light and heavy cavalry to form flying columns that can confound the enemy with lightning attacks. They are capable of fighting on horseback when necessary but they are not true cavalry and only a foolish commander uses them that way. If dragoons have a downside it's that some of their soldiers must remain with the horses once the unit dismounts. Usually one out of every five dragoons is on this duty, meaning the unit is almost never able to use its full strength when fighting on foot. Some units bring grooms with them to watch the horses, but such non-combatants are vulnerable in the situations dragoons often find themselves in.

LIGHT CHARIOTS

I guided my wolf over the hill and there before me I saw elf chariots streaming out of the forest. Elves in chariots – was I really seeing this? Did I drink too much fire water last night? Did the Smite-Father hit me upside the head?

Marguz, Goblin Wolf Archer

Chariots are a weapon of war that featured heavily in the early annals of the elves but are rarely used today. The only place chariots are found in any numbers is among the green elves, but even they mostly use them for sporting competitions. In the great glades sometimes found in wood elf lands, there are traditionally chariot races to celebrate the first day of summer. Generally, the green elves try to use the claustrophobic nature of the forests to their advantage in times of war, which usually rules out the large areas of flat terrain best for chariots. There are times, however, when chariots still race into the fray.

Battles do happen from time to time in the aforementioned glades. In the rare cases when green elf armies sally forth from their homelands, they sometimes march into terrain quite suitable for chariots. In these cases the light chariots are crewed and used in battle. Their primary role is that of mobile shooting platform. Elven chariots are designed for two crew, one driver and one archer. Units of light chariots race about the field, sending arrows into the enemy and then moving away. Sometimes the chariots are also used to quickly deploy units of foot archers. Each chariot picks up one archer from the foot troops and carries them quickly to where they are needed. The chariot archers cover them with shots while the foot archers form up. Then they speed away to carry on with their own activities. If needed, they can recover the foot archers and bring them back to the main battle line.

WAR MACHINES

Elf war machines are functional enough, certainly better than those orc pieces of junk. And of course they are pretty to look at because that's what elves like to waste their time on. Do they have the precision engineering of dwarf war machines though? I think not!

Rorik, Dwarf Engineer

The gold elves were the first of the kindred to develop war machines. From there they spread to the high elves, who needed such weapons to fulfil their dreams of conquest, and later the sea elves, who used them to arm their ships. The moon elves eschew war machines, perhaps in part because their traitorous dark elf brethren have embraced them. Green elves use war machines on occasion but they do not fit well with their style of warfare.

Elf eagles take war machines to field battles infrequently. They are slow to transport and set up, and elf generals prefer a quicker tempo of warfare. They are most often used to defend elf fortifications or to attack those of the enemy. Gold elf cities are bristling with war machines, and high elf cities are not far behind.

The most common elf war machine is the ballista, which is essentially an enormous crossbow that shoots spears across the battlefield. The spearheads can be covered in pitch, converting them into flaming weapons at a cost of some loss of accuracy. Sea elf crews do this routinely in their naval battles, as ships are large targets and fire a deadly weapon.

The elf ballista has two variants: heavy and light. The heavy ballista is large enough that it is essentially immobile. It is used as a siege weapon or mounted on ships and needs a crew of five or six. Those eagles that do bring war machines to the field favor the light ballista. They only require a crew of two or three elves to operate and have proved useful when facing monstrous foes like trolls. The elven gift of marksmanship is apparent in all the ballista crews. The dwarves may have ballistas that shoot faster, but elf ballistas are incredibly accurate.

In sieges elf engineers build trebuchets, large stone throwers that use a counter-weight mechanism. These well-designed machines can hurl rocks that weigh hundreds of pounds at walls and towers and inflict punishing damage. Trebuchets are large, heavy, and immobile, and they require large crews to operate efficiently.

MONSTROUS ALLIES

It was a bright and cloudless day but suddenly we were in shadow. I looked up and there was a griffon dropping from the sky! It crushed a half dozen men and then tore into the survivors with claws and beak. We ran and the neighboring units followed us. No amount of gold was enough to face that thing.

Bergliot, Human Mercenary

In ancient times the elves made pacts with some of the more intelligent monstrous races. Even in those days it was uncommon to see creatures like griffons, giant eagles, and dragons fighting alongside elven armies but they played an important role in several famous battles and these deeds are still frequent topics of poetry and song. These days monstrous allies on the battlefield are a rare sight indeed for two reasons. First, the numbers of such creatures has dwindled over the millennia. Second, there are few living wizards who are skilled in this sort of a magic. Summoning a monstrous ally requires the use of a magical ritual keyed to the ancient pacts. An elven wizard must both know the appropriate ritual and know the name and location of a suitable creature. This information can be hard to come by. Still, it does happen from time to time that a mighty griffon or fire-spewing dragon arrives on the battlefield to aid the elf kindred. Such creatures cannot be controlled, so commanders must be agile when a monstrous ally appears and take best advantage of the havoc they wreak.

VELLADOR ALLIES

Our ancestors swore mighty oaths to the elven kingdoms. We had to cross the mountains and fight our way through two armies but we are here. The Vellador do not take their oaths lightly.

Caralorgas, General of the Seven Cities

In ancient times the elves made alliances with human tribes that had proved themselves loyal and trustworthy. In exchange for aiding the elves in the battle, these tribes received gifts. At first these were simply implements of war; armor and weapons finer than anything the humans could make for themselves. Over time the elves passed on something even more valuable: knowledge. They taught the humans engineering, philosophy, and even some magic. These tribes went on to found their own cities and countries that were, while heavily influenced by elven thought, still of human character. The elves dubbed these humans Vellador, which translates roughly to "our civilized cousins." The Vellador often refer to themselves as "high men" and consider themselves superior to other humans (see Cullador Allies following).

The Vellador have long been tied to the elves by treaties of friendship and alliance. They can be relied upon to provide troops to the elves in times of need and receive elven help in return. They are most commonly allied with high elves, but alliances with sea elves and gold elves are known. Since the Vellador have benefited from centuries of elven military training, their armies tend to look quite similar to those of the high elves. They have equivalents to most elven troop types and in most situations will send a well-balanced army of infantry and cavalry to their allies.

The elves trust the Vellador and this manifests itself in some important ways. First, Vellador troops are allowed inside elven cities and fortresses, which is a rare honor. Second, elven generals value these troops and do not squander their lives casually. They want the Vellador to come the next time their aid is needed.

CULLADOR ALLIES

The orcs charged our line three times that day. Some sea elf swordsmen stood with us but the rest of the elves were engaged elsewhere. I lost half my command in one afternoon but there was no way we were going to let the orcs break through. I wanted the elves to see what so-called barbarians could do.

Hegener, Human Commander

The Vellador are valued but their numbers are relatively small. There are many more human tribes, cities, and nations out there who never received elven tutelage. They are called the Cullador, which roughly translates to "our barbarian cousins." Many Cullador cities are quite advanced and they resent what they see as elvish snobbery. They also reject the implication that they are "low men" compared to the Vellador. In any case, the elves still trade and form alliances with nearby human settlements, as they often have common enemies.

For elf generals Cullador troops provide the numbers that their armies lack. Elves are skilled soldiers but their numbers are not great. Cullador troops can help redress the balance when fighting armies like the orcs. For this reason the allied troops the elves value most are simple foot soldiers. Blocks of spearmen, swordsmen, and crossbowmen are useful for reinforcing the battle line. It would be unfair to say that elven generals do not value Cullador lives, but it must be said that their casualties are a secondary concern.

Cullador troops are often used to guard lines of march and communication, but unlike the Vellador they are not allowed into elven cities and fortresses. Cities have fallen at the hands of traitors before, and elf leaders do not want to take any chances. It is possible for Cullador to be elevated to the status of Vellador through loyal service, but this is rare.

ELF STRATEGIES
AND TACTICS

Elves have been waging war for countless millennia. The high elves sought it out, sending armies of conquest hither and yon. The dark elves tore their race apart in the Kin-War. All the kindred have had to deal with invaders and tyrants set on their destruction. As the elves are inveterate writers and record keepers, there is a body of military knowledge that stretches back to antiquity. The military academies delve deep into this lore when teaching their officers. Even those who never see such an academy learn of famous elven battles and heroes. They are celebrated in song and poetry, and dramatized on the stage during holiday festivities. When elves fight, they draw on their long history of both victories and defeats to inform their strategies and tactics. While not all the kindred make war in the same way, there are some common methods they all share. This chapter provides an overview of elf strategies, battlefield tactics, and naval tactics.

ELF STRATEGIES

Elves have two primary strategic goals that are frequently in conflict with one another. First, elves try to keep their number of war dead to a minimum. Since elves can live for up to 300 years, young elves dying in battle are making a huge sacrifice. The death of a 50 year old human is sad; the death of a 50 year old elf is a tragedy. Only in truly dire situations do elf armies put it all on the line. Generals are willing to temporarily cede territory and lose resources if it means keeping more soldiers alive. Retreating behind the impressive fortifications of cities and fortresses is often the smart play. Towers and walls save lives and it is often better to let the enemy batter themselves bloody than fight a field battle. Last stands and forlorn hopes are sometimes dictated by the grim realities of war, but elf generals always seek other solutions first.

The preciousness of (elf) life has driven advances in medicine and healing that feature prominently in elf eagles. Each talon has at least one and usually three healers as an integrated part of the unit. They are on the battlefield to treat the wounded and save as many as possible. A great aid to this was the invention of an herbal potion known as the Kiss of the

Moon Queen. A swallow of this concoction puts an elf into a trance state that slows down bodily functions. This makes it much less likely that wounded soldiers will bleed to death on the field. Those who survive a battle have an excellent chance of recovery under the care of the master healers. Generals know that ceding the field to adversaries like orcs is a death sentence for the wounded.

The elves' second strategic goal also has its roots in their longevity. Humans (never mind orcs) are often short-sighted. They gratify themselves today and don't think about tomorrow. Elves try to take the long view, and this most certainly applies to the way they make war. When the eagles march, the ensuing battles must be more than a short-term solution. Elf leaders go to war with the goal of permanently ending a threat if at all possible. Sometimes this can be achieved by winning a single overwhelming victory but it is not always that simple. It is often not enough to defeat an invading army. The leadership that drove it to war must be eliminated or its homeland conquered or razed. The important thing for the elves is that they do not have to fight the same enemy every five or ten years.

On first blush, this strategy sounds vicious and it can be. Elven leaders, however, don't look only to military solutions. If they can turn a defeated enemy into a trading partner or an ally, they are happy to do so. Long term alliances with many dwarf city-states and human kingdoms began with wars. Now some enemies – dark lords, orcs, and the like – cannot be made into allies. They must be either defeated totally, or re-directed elsewhere. Bloodying their noses with costly defeats and manipulating them with spycraft can often cause such enemies to seek easier prey or (better yet) fight amongst themselves. These foes are not forgotten about, however. Their activities are watched, and key players are manipulated or pushed into the most foolish and destructive decisions. The end result should be the same: the threat is eliminated.

As you can see, the twin goals of saving elf lives and ending threats permanently are not always going to be harmonious. Generals often must spend lives now to save them in the long term. They do not do this lightly. They know that their dead soldiers are sacrificing their own futures so other elves will have the opportunity to live long, full lives.

BATTLEFIELD TACTICS

While elves are often willing to let their fortifications frustrate attacking enemies, field battles are an almost inevitable part of every war. This is what the eagles train for year after year. When the time for battle comes, units have long practice maneuvering as part of a larger army. Training and discipline are both required to utilize the tactics that follow.

AMBUSH

Pointy ears are running! Follow me over the bridge. There are skulls to crush!
Final words of Dagrud Skullkrusher, Orc Warchief

This is the oldest of all elf battle tactics. It has its roots in the hunting techniques of the early tribes. To kill an animal before it bounds away, a hunter must lure it to the killing ground, surprise it, and strike before it can react. Those same principles apply to the ambush in war. While elves are hardly alone in using ambush tactics, their natural stealth and their skill at archery make them expert practitioners. It's also a tactic that can be used by forces of all size, from the small scouting party to the raiding force to the full blown army. Green elves and moon elves in particular rely on ambushes in warfare, though all the kindred use the tactic.

The first part of a successful ambush is the lure. This is often a unit of troops that seems to be retreating but in reality is leading the enemy where the elves want them to go. Sometimes the terrain itself guides attacking forces to the desired location. Next is the killing field, the place the ambush will be sprung. In many elven lands, good locations are not just chosen in advance but cultivated. Green elves create paths that lead to

clearings surrounded by undergrowth, for example, and the secret ways to hidden gold elf cities are replete with ambush sites. The chosen site must include ample cover for the elves to conceal themselves and little to no cover for the attackers.

When the enemy is fully enmeshed in the trap, a signal is given and the archers let loose. This is a moment of great confusion for the ambushed, as arrows seem to fly from nowhere to kill and wound. It is at this point that the final piece of the puzzle should drop into place. If terrain allows its concealment, a blocking force now moves behind the enemy force. Typically these will be spearmen or swordsmen, backed up with more archers if possible. When enemy troops flee from the ambush site, they run into a wall of formed troops blocking the way. Now hemmed in, foes can be destroyed or taken prisoner unless a successful breakout can be organized. Light cavalry, if available, can run down enemy troops that manage to escape from the ambush.

The green elves' use of the ambush is at its most deadly when they are defending their home forests. In these situations, they do not set up a single ambush, but a whole series of ambushes meant to wear down the invading army's numbers and morale. In addition to the scouts and archers that feature in all elf armies, they have the tree runners, who can rain death down on the enemy from the forest canopy. Fighting in this environment can be an entirely dispiriting experience for the invaders. The green elves may lead enemy troops on for days or even weeks, whittling them away with ambush after ambush until they use their full force to crush the remains of the enemy army entirely.

ARROW STORM

Archers, you have your targets. On my command, loose!
Teralel, Elf Captain

Elf armies contain a higher percentage of missile troops than any other army. Oftentimes, half an army's soldiers will be bowmen, so it only makes sense that archery is at the center of one of the most common of elven tactics. An arrow storm is exactly what it sounds like: volley after volley of arrows crashing down on the enemy battle line. When executed properly, an arrow storm can cripple and break the enemy before the armies even meet blade to blade. It sounds like a simple tactic (shoot lots of arrows; win!) but there is more to it than that.

First, the battlefield must be conducive to archery. The missile units need to be able to see what they are shooting at and the enemy should have little cover to take advantage of. If it is possible to put out ranging stakes before the enemy takes the field, so much the better. Second, the elf force must be well-supplied with arrows. An archer taking aimed shots can empty a quiver in just a few minutes and typically goes into battle with two full quivers. This is enough for a short engagement but for a proper arrow storm more ammunition is needed. The general must ensure it is available. Each talon needs a

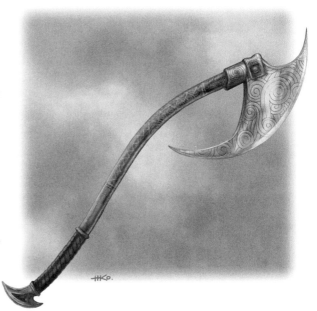

dedicated wagon parked behind it so a constant supply of fresh arrows can be provided to the unit. If fighting in defensive works, it's even easier to have stockpiled arrows at hand. Lastly, the units of archers must be deployed appropriately. Generally, that means interspersing units of archers evenly across the battle line, so a good coverage can be achieved. Some battle plans may involve concentrating on certain segments of the enemy line, and then an uneven deployment of units is necessary.

A general using the arrow storm tactic is like a conductor and the army is his orchestra. There will be points in which the best tactic is to have all archer units shooting at the closest enemy targets. Those are the crescendos. In between those there are smaller movements though. A general might open up with only one wing to counter-attacking cavalry, have only the center shoot to encourage the enemy flanks into foolish attacks, or concentrate all shooting on the center of the enemy line. Coordinating these attacks under battlefield conditions is challenging, but elves commonly handle it through signal arrows. The general keeps a talon of archers around him with a variety of signal arrows ready to fire. On his mark the whistling arrows can indicate fresh orders and new targets.

When the general judges that enough damage has been inflicted upon the enemy army, the melee troops can begin their advance. As they move out, the archers maintain their fire, so enemy units will be disrupted when the elves charge home. It takes tremendous discipline on the part of the melee troops to march towards an arrow storm, and true marksmanship on the part of the archers to keep their arrows on target as their own troops get right up on the enemy.

THE DRAGON'S SCALES

When the orc horde came into view, my mouth went dry. Its numbers seemed endless. How could we defeat an army that large? Then I looked behind me and saw thousands of elves ready for the fight. Up the slope were swordsmen and foot knights to support us. On top of the hill were rank upon rank of archers, just waiting for the command to loose. And all around me spearmen, shoulder to shoulder with shields locked. I smiled then, for I knew the dragon's scales would protect me.

Arafel, Elf Spearman

The Dragon's Scales is the standard method of deployment used by high elf eagles and from it several tactics derive. Out in front of the battle lines are skirmishing archers. They are there to neutralize enemy skirmishers and discomfort the enemy's battle line if possible. Behind them the eagle is arrayed in three separate lines. The front line is made up of spearmen in a shield wall formation. Their spears allow them to deal with both cavalry and infantry. Companions, if available, are also placed here in support of the spearmen. The middle line is primarily made up of swordsmen. Their job is to contain and push back any enemy forces that break through the front line. If the eagle contains foot knights, they are often deployed in the center of the middle line and provide the hardest hitting counter-attack. The rear line consists of formed units of archers. Their job is to shoot volleys of arrows over the heads of their comrades to thin out the enemy battle line. Units can also be detached to help neutralize breakthroughs or deal with flank attacks. If the third line can be placed on elevated terrain, so much the better. Anchoring the eagle's flanks are the cavalry. Most generals include a mix of light and heavy cavalry on each wing, though other configurations are possible. Some battles have been fought with heavy cavalry on one flank and light cavalry on the other, or with all the cavalry on one flank because the other is anchored on a river, swamp, or other impassable terrain.

The ensuing formation is a flexible one, able to deal with a variety of enemies and useful on the attack or in defense. When attacking all three lines advance while the light cavalry surges forward to pelt the enemy battle line with arrows in concert with the skirmishers. They may also engage or (even better) lead off enemy cavalry. On the general's command, the rear line stops and its archers begin shooting their volleys. Meanwhile, the first two lines continue forward until they can charge. At this point the heavy cavalry seeks openings on the flanks. If they can drive home a charge while the enemy battle line is already engaged with the infantry, the battle can usually be won. If the heavy cavalry is countered by enemy cavalry or another blocking force, the first two lines must carry the day. Alternatively, the heavy cavalry can be used to make the first charge and punch into the enemy battle line, and then the infantry can follow up and exploit its success.

The Dragon's Scales method is, if anything, even better for defense. Since the archers don't have to move forward, they can begin to shoot as soon as the enemy gets in their effective range. The light cavalry can try to goad rash units into charging ahead of their comrades and exposing themselves to destruction without proper support. The spearmen can set themselves to receive the charge and a ready shield wall is difficult to shift. Heavy cavalry can be used for flanking movements or held back to counter dangerous breakthroughs. If the general knows a defensive battle is to be fought, light ballistas may even be deployed on the flanks for added punch.

THE WYVERN'S STING

What do you mean there's elf cavalry behind us? That is not possible! Have you been into my brandy again?

General Edgerton, (disgraced) Consort of the Iron Queen

The Wyvern's Sting is a common tactic used when eagles have time and room to maneuver. It takes its name from an old saying:

If you only watch the wyvern's maw, it's the sting that will kill you.

It means that you can't become fixated on one thing or you won't see the real danger approaching. The elves refer to the various envelopment tactics they employ as the Wyvern's Sting because they rely on striking where the enemy least expects it.

At its most basic this tactic involves sending a fast moving force on a flank march while the main force keeps the attention of the enemy army fixed upon it. It is important that this flanking force stay away from prying eyes, so setting out at night is common. Special care must be taken to evade or neutralize enemy scouts while on the move. If the flanking force is detected, a canny general will escape the trap or set one of his one. If all goes well, the flanking force can attack the enemy army in its flank or rear once it has engaged the main force. Alternately, it can attack the enemy's camp or supply depots and create havoc in the rear. Trapping an army between two forces after destroying its supplies can lead to a quick victory.

Some generals have had success using more than one flanking force. This is much more difficult to coordinate. Having multiple smaller commands opens them up to being attacked and defeated one by one. Generals that have succeeded in double envelopments have become rightly famous for their victories.

Elf generals have had success with the all-mounted flanking force. This usually consists of light cavalry, heavy cavalry, and dragoons. Such a flying column is very fast indeed and can quickly wrong foot the enemy. All infantry forces can also work if the soldiers are well-trained and take only what they need with them. Campaigns that take place by the water open the possibility of troop movement by ship or boat. Sea elves obviously excel at this type of maneuver and have landed many a flanking force behind enemy lines.

NAVAL TACTICS

Although water travel is not the exclusive province of the sea elves, they are the masters of it. Sea elves maintain large fleets of vessels of all sorts and have used them to explore, trade, and make war throughout the ages. While elves use a dizzying array of boats and ships throughout their realms, when

it comes to naval warfare the sea elves have developed three ships that make up the core of their battle fleets. The lightest ships are known as falcons. They are built for speed and use only sails for propulsion. Falcons are scout ships with small crews. Their job is to find enemy ships, not engage them. The primary fighting ships are called sea serpents. They have two banks of oars and two masts, and usually carry 40 marines and 20 archers, though more can be deployed for some loss of speed. Sea serpents carry one heavy ballista in the prow but their primary method of combat is the boarding action. The heaviest ships are known as dragon turtles. They are large and tall ships, solidly constructed and difficult to sink, with three banks of oars and two masts. They have heavy ballistas fore and aft, and two light ballistas each on the port and starboard sides. Dragon turtles are the slowest elven ships but they are designed to be missile platforms. In addition to their ballistas, they usually have 100 archers on board, and a further 50 marines with long spears to repel boarders. Since they ride high and the marines are experts with their spears, dragon turtles are hard to board.

THE COILS OF THE SERPENT

Archers, I want that deck swept clean. The marines should be able to walk to the hold on a carpet of corpses by the time you are through!

Rafiel, Captain of the Golden Heron

When the goal is to capture enemy ships – for supplies, treasure, intelligence, or just the challenge – sea elves use a tactic called the Coils of the Serpent. Sea serpents typically go hunting in groups of three, sometimes with a falcon to help them find prey. They are fast ships and can overtake most merchant and war ships. Those that can't be caught with speed alone can be maneuvered into a box. Once the sea serpents have their target penned in, two of the ships concentrate on missile fire. They fire their ballistas and shoot arrows at the enemy crew while the third ship closes to board. Sailors throw out grappling hooks and pull the ships together, then the marines board the enemy ship. If the support ships have done their jobs, the marines should have an easy fight. Should things not go as planned, a second sea serpent can come alongside and disgorge its own marines. This is usually enough to finish the job.

In larger engagements, it isn't always possible to employ such favorable odds in boarding actions. If more than a half dozen ships are going to be involved, the sea elves try to bring a dragon turtle with them to provide a heavier weight of fire. This can be tricky, as dragon turtles are slower than sea serpents. If the enemy ships are faster than the dragon turtles, the tactics must change. Sometimes the sea serpents will drive enemy ships into the waiting embrace of the dragon turtles and so trap them. Another option is to use a single dragon turtle as bait, hoping to draw in enemy ships who can't resist such a prize. Once engaged, the enemy ships can be ambushed by the lurking sea serpents.

THE DRAGON'S BREATH

Where's the fleet, your majesty? Burned…all burned…

Xerto, Royal Observer

In times of war there are naval engagements in which the elves' goal is a simple one: destroy the enemy fleet. There is no faster way to do that than fire. When the battle plan is to unleash the Dragon's Breath, the sea serpents and dragon turtles must be prepared. Extra archers need to be deployed to each ship. Barrels of oil or pitch must be loaded to make fire arrows and ballista bolts. Braziers must be brought onto the ships and bolted to the decks to light them. Barrels of sand must also be loaded and fire drills rehearsed. While the plan is to make the enemy fleet burn, a bunch of ships loaded with oil, pitch, and open flames are accidents waiting to happen. All those extra supplies make the ships slower than normal. For this reason a third of the sea serpents sail with their normal equipment and crew. They provide speed and a quick reaction force when necessary.

Once the falcons have spotted the enemy, the elven fleet heads toward it. If the enemy fleet tries to escape, the unladen sea serpents shoot ahead and try to engage it until the rest of the fleet can come up. If the enemy fleet wants to fight, the unladen sea serpents move to the flanks and the rest of the fleet engages. As the two fleets approach, the elves let their fiery missiles fly. The dragon turtles are key to this tactic because they can direct a punishing barrage on any ship in range. While other navies also use war machines and flaming missiles, the real advantage the elves have is their archers. The elven longbow can shoot farther than any other bow or crossbow, so literally thousands of flaming arrows can rain down on the enemy fleet before they can answer in kind. The result is ship after ship going up like oil soaked rags. Those that escape can be hunted down by the falcons and the unladen sea serpents.

THE GRIFFON'S WINGS

As the Serellian fleet searched for us in vain, we sailed into their harbor and left their docks and warehouses in ruins.

Evatal, Captain of the Sea's Embrace

While the Dragon's Breath is a brutal and effective tactic, the fleet that employs it runs a lot of risks as well. Oftentimes, the sea elves prefer to achieve their goals by avoiding a big showdown. To do this they use the speed and maneuverability of their ships to best advantage. When the decision has been made to use the Griffon's Wings, the dragon turtles stay in port or are used to defend strategic points. Meanwhile, the rest of the fleet takes to the sea.

The falcons fan out, scouting out the route the sea serpents plan to take. Their job is not to bring the fleets together but to keep them apart. Sometimes this means leading enemy ships away, which can be dangerous for them. Meanwhile, the sea serpents make for their goal and what this is can vary. They may raid enemy ports, plunder merchant convoys, sink unprotected troop ships, or land marines and other troops in support of a land campaign. Even without facing an enemy fleet, this approach still has its challenges. There are port defenses, garrisons, unknown nautical hazards, and other problems to deal with. All the while there is the danger of the detection and enemy ships coming to attack them when they don't have the dragon turtles for heavy support.

SIEGE TACTICS

There are many bloody sieges in elven history and although they are able practitioners, it is not the elves' preferred form of warfare. They leave such tedium to the dwarves, whose temperament is better suited for it. If they must be involved in siege warfare, they much prefer to be the defenders. Elven defenses are cunningly constructed and a small force can hold out against many times its number. When elves attack, the tactic they try to avoid is the escalade. Orcs and humans may be eager to throw themselves onto prepared defenses and die in droves, but to elf generals this is a last resort. The price is simply too high in all but the most dire of situations.

If they must take a fortress or city, their preferred method is a surprise attack. Speed and boldness can often win the day before the threat is even understood. Such attacks often include sending small advanced forces like scouts and moon elf infiltrators to find hidden entrances or capture gate houses. Fast moving forces can then be inside before defenders can even muster, eliminating the need for a siege altogether.

If such a coup de main can't be mounted or does not succeed, then the attacking army will begin digging siege lines and invest the fortress or city. The besieged are then cut off from all aid and left to rot. Sometimes the goal is simply to keep the defenders bottled up while the elf army runs rampant elsewhere. In that case the besiegers only need to be strong enough to keep the cordon tight. If capitulation is necessary and there is time, the elves try to starve the defenders into submission. This can be a long process, and the elves need to be vigilant to breakout attempts from within and relief efforts from without. If the elves have one or more wizards with the army, they may not even need to wait for the defenders to starve. The siege only needs to last long enough for the wizards to cast a suitable ritual. This can be a matter of weeks for a localized effect like a section of wall tumbling down or fouling of wells, or months for more destructive effects like an earthquake or the re-routing of a river to undermine the walls.

ELF VICTORIES

The oldest existing book of elven history, *The Chronicle of Leaf and Stone*, begins with a battle, so war is something all too familiar to the elf kindred. The eons are studded with martial moments of shining glory and tragic heartbreak. A scribe could fill a dozen tomes with tales of elven arms and still there would be more to tell. In this book we must be more selective. It details five battles, one for each of the elf kindred. Each engagement is a famous victory that illustrates the methods and tactics elves use when they go to war.

BATTLE OF THE QUEEN'S EYE

In the depths of an ancient wood is a lake that shines like a mirror in the moonlight. On an island in its center is a stone circle, used for ages in the religious rituals of the elven priesthood. In bygone days green elf clans had roamed the wood but moved on or died out and eventually the only kindred who still came there were the moon elves. On certain nights they could commune with the Moon Queen, and show her that her people honored her still.

For the most part the moon elves had little trouble traveling through the forest to the lake they called the Queen's Eye. One year Valantel, a priestess of the Moon Queen, led her clan to the forest in anticipation of the ritual. Her scouts reported something most troubling: a tribe of gnolls had settled around the lake. Gnolls, fearsome hyena-headed humanoids, were not native to the region. A wizard named Ul'Carnek had brought them here from the north. He was working his own ritual in the stone circle. Valantel didn't know the nature of this ritual but she could not afford to wait and find out. The moon would be full in a matter of days and the Queen's Eye needed to be reclaimed by then.

Valantel conferred with her clan's chief, Meandor. They mustered their warriors and then sent the noncombatants a safe distance away. Their force numbered but a hundred, a mix of swordsmen, archers, scouts, and infiltrators. The gnolls had at least three times as many fighters. Getting them away from the Queen's Eye would not be an easy task.

The following night the moon elves moved into position around the gnoll encampment. The gnolls were not expecting trouble and had only a few sentries posted. The infiltrators took care of them quickly and quietly. Then Valantel led a dozen infiltrators under the docks. When they were in place and ready, an archer fired a signal arrow whose whistle sounded like a forest bird. This was Meandor's signal.

Arrows filled the air and plunged down on the sleeping gnolls. They awoke in confusion, as Meandor's scouts and archers continued to shoot withering volleys. In the camp all was confusion until the gnoll chieftain began to pull his warriors together. Gnoll archers began to fire blindly into the trees while the chieftain got his axemen into a shield wall. This he advanced towards the treeline at a quick pace, even as elven arrows continued to rain down upon them. As the majority of the gnolls moved away from their camp, Valantel and the infiltrators commandeered small boats and began to row to the island.

In the woods the moon elf scouts and archers began to fall back, leading the gnolls away from their camp. The gnolls had their scent now and packs of them split off to pursue small groups of archers. With their quickness and ferocity, the gnolls overwhelmed some of the archers. Other packs were led into waiting units of swordsmen, who ambushed the gnolls and then faded back into the forest. Meandor and his warriors continued to bleed the gnolls until the chieftain had had enough and called the retreat back to camp.

Meanwhile, Valantel and the infiltrators reached the Queen's Eye and made their way to the stone circle. There Ul'Carnek was performing a ritual around a great fire. His bodyguard of 20 gnolls were with him, along with a towering ogre who helped enforce the wizard's will. The gnolls had heard the sounds of battle and were on edge. Quarrels fired from hand crossbows flew out of the darkness. They were small but the moon elves had dipped them in potent venom.

Soon the wizard's bodyguards were crashing to the ground and convulsing as the poison tore through their systems. Then the infiltrators were among them with their short, deadly blades.

Ul'Carnek was shaken from his mystical trance and saw carnage all about him. He pulled out a wand and fired a blast of ice that froze one infiltrator in his tracks. The ogre smashed another to the ground with his great club. Two more infiltrators engaged the ogre with crescent staves. One kept its attention while the other used her weapon to sever the ogre's tendons. The monster came crashing down and the flashing crescent blades ended its life. Ul'Carnek tried his wand on Valantel but could only stare wide-eyed as she walked through the cloud of ice. "The Moon Queen is my shield!" she shouted, as her blade took Ul'Carnek's head from his shoulders.

When the gnoll chieftain and his warriors returned to the camp they found the heads of Ul'Carnek and his ogre mounted on spears in front of a roaring fire. The survivors fled and did not return. The following night Valantel performed her own ritual and it is said the Moon Queen spoke to her people for the first time in decades. What she said the moon elves will never repeat.

SIEGE OF AVELORN

After he had crushed a human army, the orc warlord Shadderak found himself with a number of prisoners. Most went right into the stewpot but one yammered on in broken orcish that he had a valuable secret. The warlord sent for his shaman to translate and Shadderak interrogated the prisoner. The human, a mercenary named Ruderick, claimed that he knew the location of one of the hidden gold elf cities. Unbelievable plunder could be Shadderak's, but only if he kept Ruderick alive and let him go once he guided to the orcs to the elf city. The orc warlord did like the idea of killing a lot of elves and taking their shiny stuff, so he let Ruderick live. For the time being anyway. He turned the human over to his scouts and told them to lead the horde to the hidden city.

The horde marched for several weeks, eventually approaching a mountain range. As they got closer, units of elven light cavalry began hit and run attacks on the horde. They rode up, unleashed volleys of arrows, and raced away. Shadderak's wolf riders gamely pursued them and always the elves tried to pull them south. Ruderick insisted the correct course was east so the horde kept on its path. It seemed as if only sheer cliff was to their front but this proved an optical illusion. There was a gorge that led into the mountains. The city was that way, claimed Ruderick.

The horde marched up the gorge. Now elf infantry began to attack from above, shooting arrows and dropping stones. A wiser general would have retreated but now Shadderak's blood was up and he kept driving the orcs forward despite casualties. Eventually the gorge widened out into a small valley and there was an elven fortress. It seemed small for a city but Ruderick said that much of the city was underground. This made sense to the orc warlord, so he deployed the horde and began making siege lines.

The fortress was called Avelorn and its commander the battle-tested General Ullator. He had perhaps 500 gold elf soldiers and Shadderak's horde numbered at least 4,000. Ullator sent out messengers for aid before Avelorn was invested and then set about planning his defense with his captains. His greatest advantage was that Avelorn was a training depot for the Knights of the Chalice so fully a third of his troops were heavy infantry. The remainder were spearmen, swordsmen, and archers, and the light cavalry that had tried and failed to redirect the horde. The fortress also had four ballistas mounted on its towers.

Shadderak had brought disassembled war machines with him, and the orcs began to construct the catapults and ballistas. Meanwhile, one of his warchiefs, Krimbaz, loudly proclaimed that he could take the fortress with an immediate assault. Shadderak knew that the warchief was a threat to his position so he ordered the assault and let Krimbaz lead it. The canny

warlord knew an unsupported escalade would fail, so he held back his better troops. The elves filled the attackers with arrows and threw down their ladders. Krimbaz and most of his warband were killed and Shadderak had one problem less. Soon the orc war machines, creaky though they might be, were throwing stones at the fortress. The orcs also readied a large battering ram.

At first Ullator was unconcerned about the orc war machines. They were poorly constructed and inaccurate, and it would take them some time to knock down one of Avelorn's walls or towers. Then a lucky shot hit the front gate and damaged it heavily. This was a worrisome development because Ullator needed time more than anything else. That night Ullator led a sortie out of the fortress with the aim of destroying the war machines. The elves made good progress at first, cutting down many orcs and firing several of the machines. Shadderak responded quickly though and soon the elves had to retreat or get cut off by the orcs' superior numbers.

Ullator had his engineers repair the gate as best they could, and then had them construct barricades in the courtyard beyond. One hundred Knights of the Chalice were quartered nearby. Shadderak meanwhile brooded over his smoldering catapults. The elves hadn't destroyed them all but it would take more time than he wanted to spend to knock down a wall. He had seen what happened to the gate though, and decided that was his way forward. He spent a day re-organizing his horde and then planned an attack for the following day.

That morning the catapults began shooting early. Shadderak ordered them to aim for the gate this time. This proved more difficult than he had predicted, and the horde stood ready all morning and into the afternoon as the catapults missed their target. Finally, as the sun started towards the horizon, a second stone hit the gate and shuddered it. That's what Shadderak had been waiting for. He signaled for an immediate attack.

Orc warbands picked up their siege ladders and moved out. Goblin archers ran ahead and tried to keep the elf archers' heads down. They were only partially successful and soon volleys of arrows were falling on the orcs. Ballista bolts flew from the towers, often skewering two or three orcs at a time. Opposite the gate Shadderak had formed up his Ironbackers, great orcs in plate armor with heavy shields, and they advanced with the battering ram. The warrior infantry got to the wall first and the siege ladders went up. A fierce struggle erupted, as elf spearmen sought to push the ladders off the wall or stab the orcs as they swarmed up. The gold elves were holding the wall but their casualties began to rise. Elf captains called for Ullator to send Knights of the

Chalice to the walls but he refused. He knew where his greatest point of weakness was.

Soon enough there was a great crash at the gate as the Ironbacks slammed their ram home. They had lost a few orcs to archery but their heavy armor and shields let them weather the worst of it. Now the Ironbacks put all their strength into the battering ram. Stones rained down on them from above but still they kept at it. Finally with one last thrust, the orcs knocked the damaged gates in. The Ironbacks roared their war cry and charged into the fortress. Waiting for them in the courtyard were a hundred Knights of the Chalice behind formidable barricades. Now the fight began in earnest. Two units of heavily armored troops locked in a death struggle. The orcs were bigger and stronger but the elves were more skilled and were fighting behind barricades. The contest continued until the sun was setting, swaying back and forth. Finally Ullator and his picked troops charged into the fray and surviving Ironbacks retreated out of the fortress. The courtyard was choked with elf and orc corpses but the gold elves had held.

Shadderak planned to renew the assault in the morning. He had been so close! He received bad news from his wolf riders, however. A large gold elf army had positioned itself outside the gorge, trapping the orcs within. Avelorn had only ever been a border fort. The great gold elf city Ruderick had mistaken it for was hidden much deeper in the mountains. It had sent an army by a different route and now Shadderak was trapped. When the warlord realized his folly, he killed Ruderick and ate his heart. Shadderak and his horde were soon crushed between the fortress and the army. Not one of them escaped to reveal Avelorn's location.

BATTLE OF THE WASTREL PRINCE

King Vlandin of the dwarf City-State of Zhorshun was a vain and paranoid ruler who alienated his own people. He suppressed the guilds and arrested those who tried to re-establish them. He also sought personal glory with a series of ill-advised military ventures. One of the most disastrous of these was King Vlandin's attack on the green elf Kingdom of Thistlewood. The trouble started when the king's son, Prince Zetrosh, visited Thistlewood. Although received and honored by the elf king, Zetrosh got drunk, made several insulting remarks, and then killed one of the king's stags with a repeating crossbow the following day. The prince was lucky he was only escorted to the edge of the forest and told to go home. Nonetheless, King Vlandin declared that the elves had

insulted his good name and swore
vengeance upon Thistlewood.
He mustered his war host and
marched to war, despite the
protestations of his
advisors. He was turning
an allied kingdom into an
enemy in defense of his
wastrel of a son. Vlandin
believed he could easily defeat
the green elves and burnish his
reputation with a conqueror's
glory.

King Cadorel of Thistlewood
found the whole situation difficult to
believe. He sent an envoy to King
Vlandin, who first beat up and then cast out
the diplomat. An infuriated Cadorel then prepared for war. The dwarves
had a long march ahead of them and the country leading to Thistlewood
was a flat, open plain. This was perfect country for cavalry – and chariots.
Cadorel dispatched his light cavalry and chariots to harass the dwarf war
host on its march. They could literally ride circles around the dwarf
column, peppering it with arrows and then speeding away. The casualties
inflicted were not great but it was demoralizing for the dwarf soldiers to
endure these attacks day in and day out. King Cadorel hoped that
Vlandin would realize his folly and return home before he got to
Thistlewood. Like many foolish men in positions beyond their ability,
however, King Vlandin brimmed with confidence. "On to Thistlewood
and victory!" he declared.

Once the war host made it to the forest, things only got worse for the
dwarves. The gnome allies they expected did not show up (the gnomes
being unwilling to sacrifice their own friendship with the green elves).
The war wagons were found to be too heavy and ponderous to navigate
inside the forest and had to be left on the outskirts. And the very nature
of the terrain made it difficult for the dwarf heavy infantry to adopt its
usual formation. The captain of the dwarf rangers told King Vlandin it
was suicide to go on. The king stripped him of his rank and left him a
prisoner with the war wagons (thus inadvertently saving the truth-teller's
life).

As the dwarves pushed into the forest, the ambushes began. Skirmisher
archers appeared as if from nowhere, poured fire into the dwarves, and
then disappeared. Tree runners rained death from above. They found

that while dwarf armor could often protect against arrows and javelins, falling stones were much more effective. The green elves then made greater efforts to haul rocks up into the forest canopy for the tree runners' use. Not everything went the elves' way, as the war host still had many skilled officers and veteran soldiers of long service. They found that grenades worked well in the forest and a fusillade from the grenadiers could take a toll from ambushers. Their repeating crossbows also began to take a toll on the tree runners, as they could produce a great volume of fire.

For a week the war host was bled from a thousand cuts and still Vlandin would not admit defeat. When King Cadorel judged the time was right, he maneuvered the war host to one of the great clearings used for chariot races in peaceful times. Here the green elves had arrayed themselves for battle, a shield wall of spearmen in front with ranks of archers behind. Vlandin was ecstatic. Now his heavy infantry could deploy properly. The elves had finally come out and now he would crush them.

The dwarves marched methodically towards the elf shield wall. Arrows arced over the spearmen to crash down upon the dwarves, but their armor and shields gave good protection. Their shields only faced forward, however, and soon the dwarves had a new problem. More elf archers appeared to the flanks of the advancing war host. Then the light cavalry burst from the trees and rode around to their rear. Soon elf arrows were falling on the dwarves from all sides. Great ragged holes appeared in their ranks but still they maintained discipline. At last they neared the elf shieldwall and then they charged.

The long spears of the elves took a toll on the charging dwarves but then the dwarves were in their element. They pushed hard on the elven battle line and it bowed inwards. The more lightly armored green elves could not stand up to dwarf shock troops for very long. The dwarf attack began to slow, however, because the rear of their formations continued to take a beating from nimble horse archers and skirmishing bowmen. The dwarf crossbowmen, out of ammunition, could offer no reply. Finally King Cadorel led his household foot knights in a charge that stopped the dwarf advance cold. First one dwarf unit then another began to beat a fighting retreat. King Vlandin raged against this "treason" but soon had no choice but to join them.

The war host that emerged from Thistlewood was a shattered wreck. King Cadorel let the dwarves retreat. Enough blood had been spilled. King Vlandin survived the disaster only to meet a different fate upon his return home. See Dwarf Warfare for further details.

BATTLE OF YAMANI'S CROSSING

South of the sea elf city-state of Telwing was an expanding human theocracy called Anuritan. Its priests were an unpleasant bunch who burned sacrifices alive to honor their savage god, Vatesh the Flame Bringer. Anuritan had conquered lands to the east, west, and south, but had never moved north. It was a land power and its attempts to challenge Telwing on the sea had all ended in disaster. Furthermore a strait separated the lands of Telwing and Anuritan and this made it difficult for the humans to bring their armies north. Getting their war elephants across the strait was a particularly thorny problem for them.

The sea elves patrolled the strait regularly and generally felt they had little to fear from Anuritan. They did not count on the drive or ingenuity of the priests of Vatesh, however. They pushed their engineers year after year until they came up with a solution to the problem of the strait. They would lash ships together and lay down a road on top of them. This would allow the army and the elephants to march into Telwing. That summer, in what the elves would call bad luck and the humans divine providence, much of Telwing's fleet was sent north to deal with a growing pirate threat. The patrols of the strait thus became infrequent. When the humans began to build their bridge of boats, it went undetected for weeks.

A falcon warship finally spotted what was happening. Human ships tried to stop it but the falcon was too fast and escaped north, carrying the news to the city of Telwing. The commander of the city-state's military, General Faylen, immediately sent light cavalry and dragoons to the crossing site, while preparing the rest of the army to march. She also sent falcons out to find all the nearby warships and order them back to Telwing.

By the time the sea elf cavalry reached the strait, the bridge of boats was almost complete. The dragoons dismounted and began to attack the engineers and crews on the bridge with their bows. The dragoon's numbers were not great, so the humans landed light infantry from small boats of their own. The elf light cavalry, concealed behind a nearby hill, now rode out and caused great mayhem among the landing troops. They shot down many and then rode among them with sabers, driving them back to their own boats. The dragoons and light cavalry kept up these tactics for three days, delaying the completion of the bridge. Finally, the human engineers built mantlets to protect the works crews. It took them a further four days to finish the bridge. As soon as it was ready, the priests sent troops across. The elves harried them with arrows as long as they could and then retreated as the bridgehead was established.

The High Priest of Anuritan, Yamani, came over the bridge with his escort of Templar cavalry. Half his army had made it across the strait and he wanted to be on hand when the elephants crossed. Meanwhile, General Faylen arrived with the main sea elf force. The stage was now set for a battle that would determine the fate of Telwing.

The next morning a sea bird arrived in camp with a message for General Faylen. She smiled and ordered the army to deploy for battle. The sea elf army advanced towards the bridgehead. High Priest Yamani deployed his own troops and sent a message to get the war elephants across immediately. This was easier said than done. It took much coaxing and prodding to get the elephants onto the bridge. By the time the first two were making their way across, the battle had been joined.

Even half the Anuritan army outnumbered that of Telwing, so Yamani was confident of victory. He had heavy cavalry in the form of his Templars and the sea elves had none. When the war elephants made it across, he would complete the destruction of the elves in the name of Vatesh the Flame Bringer. Faylen advanced her battle line. She had spearmen in front backed by companions, with archers on the flanks. Swordsmen, light cavalry, and dragoons were in reserve. Their opponents were mostly medium infantry armed with swords and axes, with supporting crossbowmen and the Templars in reserve.

The sea elves advanced and their archers began to shoot before the crossbows could possibly reply. These volleys hammered the human line, wounding and killing many of the high priest's men. Other commanders would have kept at range as long as possible but Faylen pushed her battle line forward. She wanted to hem the humans in and keep them close to shore. It soon became obvious why that was.

Cries went up on the bridge. Elven ships were bearing down on them. Faylen had only been able to get four of the larger warships here in time, one dragon turtle and three sea serpents. They sailed for the bridge at high speed. Ballistas and then archers fired as they approached, killing troops on the bridge and causing great confusion. The elephants reared and stamped. Then a figure appeared on the prow of the dragon turtle. It was the wizard Adrym. He held his staff high and two bright balls of light flew from its tip towards the bridge. When they struck it, they exploded in fiery splendor. The bridge shuddered as it broke into three

sections, pitching the war elephants and burning men into the water. Soon the whole bridge was engulfed in flame.

Yamani and his force were now trapped in Telwing territory. The two battle lines had come together and were now fighting furiously. The elves were fighting well and his men were dispirited. It was up to the Templars to save the day for Anuritan. He ordered them to flank the elven line and charge. There was only one problem. The Templars had to cross behind the melee before they could move out on the flank, and in doing so they rode by the shore. The elven warships aimed their heavy ballistas and let fly. Their huge spears skewered Templars and horses. Archers on the ships followed up and in a matter of minutes the Templars were annihilated. The sea serpents then beached themselves and marines leaped on the shore. They hit the human battle line from behind and soon the whole thing collapsed. Humans streamed back to the water line and tried to swim for home. Their own small boats rescued some. High Priest Yamani was last seen clinging to a piece of wood while being swept out to sea.

BATTLE OF BLEACHBONE PASS

The Ravillon Empire had once bestridden the continent like a colossus. The high elves had conquered region after region, ever expanding their territory. For centuries the empire remained strong but then cracks began to appear. It lost a territory here, a city-state there. There then followed a span of decades so disastrous they became known as the Dark Century. Towards the end of this period it seemed the final death was on the way. Across the Blackpeak Mountains a new leader had arisen. Her name was Morrikalli, Tyrant of Kheldrassas. She was a dark elf and a demon worshipper like all her traitorous kin. Morrikalli had come to the surface world with a few hundred dark elf warriors and over the course of 30 years had conquered all the land beyond the mountains (for details on one of these battles, see *Orc Warfare*). Ravillon would be next and there was only one way through the Blackpeaks large enough for her army: Bleachbone Pass.

Emperor Taerentin sent out the call across the empire. Although it was smaller than it had once been, he could still assemble a sizeable force. In addition to high elf units from every city, Taerentin's army included gold elf, sea elf, green elf, and Vellador contingents. They rallied in the capital and then marched towards Bleachbone Pass. Everyone knew that the pass took its name from the remains of those who had fought previous battles there. Many understood that their bones were likely to join them.

On their arrival Taerentin's army spent several days skirmishing with

Morrikalli's approaching forces. The high elves had gotten there in time to seize the most important piece of terrain inside the pass, a low hill known as Flattop. Some centuries before a high elf commander had ordered the top of the hill removed so he could better deploy his troops there. Taerentin, a keen student of history, had remembered this and brought along ballistas to emplace there. He also stationed archers on the hill and positioned his heavy cavalry out of sight behind it. In front of the hill was the might of the high elf cities. Rank after rank of spearmen, swordsmen, and companions, and in the center of the line the Knights of the Phoenix. On the right flank were the gold elf and Vellador contingents and on the left the green elf and sea elf contingents.

The first of Morrikalli's troops to arrive were orcs. She had two sworn warlords in her service, Krugash and Vaarg. Orcs were fast marchers, so she ordered Krugash ahead with his horde to test the elven line. The orc skirmishers came first, followed by warbands of warrior infantry. They attacked the left flank while the rest of Morrikalli's army deployed behind them. Arrows tore into the orcs, but soon their skirmishers were in range, throwing javelins at the elf lines. Despite great casualties, the orc infantry completed their charge and succeeded in causing some mayhem. The fighting was intense but brief, as the orcs didn't have the numbers. The sea and green elves pushed them back and the orcs retreated. The dead orcs meant nothing to Morrikalli. She was now deployed and she had made her foes spend some resources.

In the center of Morrikalli's line were her dark elf veterans and ogre mercenaries. On her right flank were the two orc hordes and on the left her human contingent, including the heavy cavalry known as the Knights of Kheldrassas. On Morrikalli's signals, braying horns echoed in the pass and her army advanced. The missile troops of both armies began their deadly exchange. Now Emperor Taerentin revealed his first surprise. On the mountains to either side of the pass, the gold elves had long ago excavated hidden galleries and these were now filled with their archers. Now the gold elves plunged arrows into the ranks of the enemy army from above and behind. These wrought a fearful slaughter and caused the wings of Morrikalli's army to pull away from the center to escape it.

Now Morrikalli had her horns sound the charge. Her army had to get to grips with the elven host or they would be shot to pieces. The orcs sped ahead, their berserkers in the lead. In the center dark elf halberdiers and ogre mercenaries charged home, while to their left the human heavy infantry fought their way forward. All across Bleachbone Pass elves, orcs, and men stabbed, bashed, and cut each other in a fearful press. Trouble soon developed on Taerentin's right wing. The Knights of Kheldrassas charged the Vellador and punched right through them. The gold elves

struggled to stem the tide. Taerentin had to release the Griffon Knights, who charged in to save their kin. They smashed the human knights and the line was restored. An orc breakthrough on the left wing similarly had to be reversed by a charge of the Star Knights.

In front of Flattop Hill the battle was at its most brutal. High elves and dark elves met in furious combat. Morrikalli's ogres, their ranks thinned by ballista fire, still took a fearful toll on the high elves. It was the Knights of the Phoenix who finally ended the threat, their great weapons chopping the remaining ogres down. Their move had created a gap in the line, however, and now the dark elf halberdiers charged into it. The high elf archers retreated up the hill and the dark elves surged forward. The archers, however, had retreated to reveal Taerentin's final surprise: moon elves! They had answered the call after all and the disorganized dark elves ran into a perfectly formed phalanx of their hated brethren. The moon elves' wrath was great as they attacked their traitorous kin. They pushed the dark elves down the hill and now infiltrators appeared on their flanks to aid in the slaughter.

Morrikalli could see that her gambit had failed and the center of her line was buckling. She had the horns sound the retreat. Many more fell to missile fire or to the light cavalry that came out to harry them, but enough of her horde survived for her to maintain power. She continued to be a menace for many years but she never again attempted to invade Ravillon. Taerentin used this hard won victory to reverse the decline of the empire and begin a resurgence that seemed unthinkable after the Dark Century.

Introduction:
Stopping to
Buy Sparknotes
on a Snowy
Evening

Whose words these are you *think* you know.
Your paper's due tomorrow, though;
We're glad to see you stopping here
To get some help before you go.

Lost your course? You'll find it here.
Face tests and essays without fear.
Between the words, good grades at stake:
Get great results throughout the year.

Once school bells caused your heart to quake
As teachers circled each mistake.
Use SparkNotes and no longer weep,
Ace every single test you take.

Yes, books are lovely, dark, and deep,
But only what you grasp you keep,
With hours to go before you sleep,
With hours to go before you sleep.

Contents

CONTEXT   1

PLOT OVERVIEW   3

CHARACTER LIST   7

ANALYSIS OF MAJOR CHARACTERS   13
 CHIEF BROMDEN   13
 RANDLE MCMURPHY   14
 NURSE RATCHED   15

THEMES, MOTIFS & SYMBOLS   17
 WOMEN AS CASTRATORS   17
 SOCIETY'S DESTRUCTION OF NATURAL IMPULSES   18
 THE IMPORTANCE OF EXPRESSING SEXUALITY   19
 FALSE DIAGNOSES OF INSANITY   20
 INVISIBILITY   21
 THE POWER OF LAUGHTER   21
 REAL VERSUS IMAGINED SIZE   22
 THE FOG MACHINE   22
 MCMURPHY'S BOXER SHORTS   22
 THE ELECTROSHOCK THERAPY TABLE   23

SUMMARY & ANALYSIS   25
 PART I   25
 PART I, CONTINUED   29
 PART II   33
 PART III   37
 PART IV   41

IMPORTANT QUOTATIONS EXPLAINED   47

KEY FACTS   53

STUDY QUESTIONS & ESSAY TOPICS   56

REVIEW & RESOURCES   60
    QUIZ   60
    SUGGESTIONS FOR FURTHER READING   65

CONTEXT

K EN KESEY WAS BORN in 1935 in La Junta, Colorado. He grew up in Oregon and returned there to teach until his death in November 2001. After being elected the boy most likely to succeed by his high school class, Kesey enrolled in the University of Oregon. He married in 1956, a year before receiving his bachelor's degree. Afterward, he won a fellowship to a creative writing program at Stanford University. While he was there, he became a volunteer in a program to test the effects of new drugs at the local Veterans Administration hospital. During this time, he discovered LSD and became interested in studying alternative methods of perception. He soon took a job in a mental institution, where he spoke extensively to the patients.

Kesey's *One Flew Over the Cuckoo's Nest* is based largely on his experiences with mental patients. Through the conflict between Nurse Ratched and Randle Patrick McMurphy, the novel explores the themes of individuality and rebellion against conformity, ideas that were widely discussed at a time when the United States was committed to opposing communism and totalitarian regimes around the world. However, Kesey's approach, directing criticism at American institutions themselves, was revolutionary in a way that would find greater expression during the sixties. The novel, published in 1962, was an immediate success.

With his newfound wealth, Kesey purchased a farm in California, where he and his friends experimented heavily with LSD. He soon became the focus of a growing drug cult. He believed that using LSD to achieve altered states of mind could improve society. Kesey's high profile as an LSD guru in the midst of the public's growing hysteria against it and other drugs attracted the attention of legal authorities. Kesey fled to Mexico after he was caught trying to flush some marijuana down a toilet. When he returned to the United States, he was arrested and sent to jail for several months.

In 1964, Kesey led a group of friends called the Merry Pranksters on a road trip across the United States in a bus named Furthur. The participants included Neil Cassady, who had also participated in the 1950s version of this trip with Jack Kerouac and company. The trip involved massive consumption of LSD and numerous subversive adventures. The exploits of the Merry Pranksters are detailed in

Tom Wolfe's *The Electric Kool-Aid Acid Test*. This book became a must-read for the hippie generation, and much of the generation's slang and philosophy comes directly from its pages.

Dale Wasserman adapted *One Flew Over the Cuckoo's Nest* into a play version that ran on Broadway in 1963, with Kirk Douglas in the leading role. In 1975, a movie version was released without Kesey's permission, directed by Milos Forman. It was extremely successful, though quite different from the novel. It was nominated for nine Academy Awards and swept the five major categories. As a result, for many people familiar with the film version, Randle McMurphy will forever be associated with Jack Nicholson, the famous actor who portrayed him.

PLOT OVERVIEW

CHIEF BROMDEN, THE HALF-INDIAN NARRATOR of *One Flew Over the Cuckoo's Nest,* has been a patient in an Oregon psychiatric hospital for ten years. His paranoia is evident from the first lines of the book, and he suffers from hallucinations and delusions. Bromden's worldview is dominated by his fear of what he calls the Combine, a huge conglomeration that controls society and forces people into conformity. Bromden pretends to be deaf and dumb and tries to go unnoticed, even though he is six feet seven inches tall.

The mental patients, all male, are divided into Acutes, who can be cured, and Chronics, who cannot be cured. They are ruled by Nurse Ratched, a former army nurse who runs the ward with harsh, mechanical precision. During daily Group Meetings, she encourages the Acutes to attack each other in their most vulnerable places, shaming them into submission. If a patient rebels, he is sent to receive electroshock treatments and sometimes a lobotomy, even though both practices have fallen out of favor with the medical community.

When Randle McMurphy arrives as a transfer from the Pendleton Work Farm, Bromden senses that something is different about him. McMurphy swaggers into the ward and introduces himself as a gambling man with a zest for women and cards. After McMurphy experiences his first Group Meeting, he tells the patients that Nurse Ratched is a ball-cutter. The other patients tell him that there is no defying her, because in their eyes she is an all-powerful force. McMurphy makes a bet that he can make Ratched lose her temper within a week.

At first, the confrontations between Ratched and McMurphy provide entertainment for the other patients. McMurphy's insubordination, however, soon stimulates the rest of them into rebellion. The success of his bet hinges on a failed vote to change the television schedule to show the World Series, which is on during the time allotted for cleaning chores. McMurphy stages a protest by sitting in front of the blank television instead of doing his work, and one by one the other patients join him. Nurse Ratched loses control and screams at them. Bromden observes that an outsider would think all of them were crazy, including the nurse.

In Part II, McMurphy, flush with victory, taunts Nurse Ratched and the staff with abandon. Everyone expects him to get sent to the Disturbed ward, but Nurse Ratched keeps him in the regular ward, thinking the patients will soon see that he is just as cowardly as everyone else. McMurphy eventually learns that involuntarily committed patients are stuck in the hospital until the staff decides they are cured. When McMurphy realizes that he is at Nurse Ratched's mercy, he begins to submit to her authority. By this time, however, he has unintentionally become the leader for the other patients, and they are confused when he stops standing up for them. Cheswick, dismayed when McMurphy fails to join him in a stand against Nurse Ratched, drowns in the pool in a possible suicide.

Cheswick's death signals to McMurphy that he has unwittingly taken on the responsibility of rehabilitating the other patients. He also witnesses the harsh reality of electroshock therapy and becomes genuinely frightened by the power wielded by the staff. The weight of his obligation to the other patients and his fear for his own life begins to wear down his strength and his sanity. Nevertheless, in Part III, McMurphy arranges a fishing trip for himself and ten other patients. He shows them how to defuse the hostility of the outside world and enables them to feel powerful and masculine as they catch large fish without his help. He also arranges for Billy Bibbit to lose his virginity later in the novel, by making a date between Billy and Candy Starr, a prostitute from Portland.

Back on the ward in Part IV, McMurphy reignites the rebellion by getting into a fistfight with the aides to defend George Sorenson. Bromden joins in, and they are both sent to the Disturbed ward for electroshock therapy. McMurphy acts as if the shock treatments do not affect him, and his heroic reputation grows. Nurse Ratched brings him back to the ward so the other patients can see his weakened state. The patients urge McMurphy to escape, but he has arranged Billy's date for that night, and he refuses to let Billy down. McMurphy bribes Mr. Turkle, the night aide, to sneak Candy into the hospital, and they have a party on the ward. Billy has sex with Candy while McMurphy and the other patients smoke marijuana and drink. Harding tries to get McMurphy to escape with Candy and Sandy to Mexico, but McMurphy is too wasted and falls asleep.

The aides discover the mess the next morning, setting off a series of violent events. When Nurse Ratched finds Billy with Candy, she threatens to tell Billy's mother. Billy becomes hysterical and commits suicide by cutting his throat. McMurphy attacks Ratched, ripping open the front of her dress and attempting to strangle her. In retaliation, she has him lobotomized, and he returns to the ward as a vegetable. However, Ratched has lost her tyrannical power over the ward. The patients transfer to other wards or check themselves out of the hospital. Bromden suffocates McMurphy in his bed, enabling him to die with some dignity rather than live as a symbol of Ratched's power. Bromden, having recovered the immense strength that he had believed lost during his time in the mental ward, escapes from the hospital by breaking through a window.

CHARACTER LIST

Chief Bromden The narrator of *One Flew Over the Cuckoo's Nest*. Chief Bromden is the son of the chief of the Columbia Indians and a white woman. He suffers from paranoia and hallucinations, has received multiple electroshock treatments, and has been in the hospital for ten years, longer than any other patient in the ward. Bromden sees modern society as a huge, oppressive conglomeration that he calls the Combine and the hospital as a place meant to fix people who do not conform. Bromden chronicles the story of the mental ward while developing his perceptual abilities and regaining a sense of himself as an individual.

Randle McMurphy The novel's protagonist. Randle McMurphy is a big, redheaded gambler, a con man, and a backroom boxer. His body is heavily scarred and tattooed, and he has a fresh scar across the bridge of his nose. He was sentenced to six months at a prison work farm, and when he was diagnosed as a psychopath—for "too much fighting and fucking"—he did not protest because he thought the hospital would be more comfortable than the work farm. McMurphy serves as the unlikely Christ figure in the novel—the dominant force challenging the establishment and the ultimate savior of the victimized patients.

Nurse Ratched The head of the hospital ward. Nurse Ratched, the novel's antagonist, is a middle-aged former army nurse. She rules her ward with an iron hand and masks her humanity and femininity behind a stiff, patronizing facade. She selects her staff for their submissiveness, and she weakens her patients through a psychologically manipulative program designed to destroy their self-esteem. Ratched's emasculating, mechanical ways slowly drain all traces of humanity from her patients.

Dale Harding An acerbic, college-educated patient and president of the Patients' Council. Harding helps McMurphy understand the realities of the hospital. Although he is married, Harding is a homosexual. He has difficulty dealing with the overwhelming social prejudice against homosexuals, so he hides in the hospital voluntarily. Harding's development and the reemergence of his individual self signal the success of McMurphy's battle against Ratched, especially when Harding checks himself out of the ward and paves the way for the other cured patients to leave.

Billy Bibbit A shy patient. Billy has a bad stutter and seems much younger than his thirty-one years. Billy Bibbit is dominated by his mother, one of Nurse Ratched's close friends. Billy is voluntarily in the hospital, as he is afraid of the outside world.

Doctor Spivey A mild-mannered doctor who may be addicted to opiates. Nurse Ratched chose Doctor Spivey as the doctor for her ward because he is as easily cowed and dominated as the patients. With McMurphy's arrival, he, like the patients, begins to assert himself. He often supports McMurphy's unusual plans for the ward, such as holding a carnival.

Charles Cheswick The first patient to support McMurphy's rebellion against Nurse Ratched's power. Cheswick, a man of much talk and little action, drowns in the pool—possibly a suicide—after McMurphy does not support Cheswick when Cheswick takes a stand against Nurse Ratched. Cheswick's death is significant in that it awakens McMurphy to the extent of his influence and the mistake of his decision to conform.

Warren, Washington, Williams, and Geever Hospital aides. Warren, Washington, and Williams are Nurse Ratched's daytime aides; Geever is the nighttime aide. Nurse Ratched hired them because they are filled with hatred and will submit to her wishes completely.

Candy Starr A beautiful, carefree prostitute from Portland. Candy Starr accompanies McMurphy and the other patients on the fishing trip, and then comes to the ward for a late-night party that McMurphy arranges.

George Sorenson A hospital patient, a big Swede, and a former seaman. McMurphy recruits George Sorenson to be captain for the fishing excursion. He is nicknamed "Rub-a-Dub George" by the aides because he has an intense phobia toward dirtiness. McMurphy's defense of George leads McMurphy to his first electroshock treatment.

Pete Bancini A hospital patient who suffered brain damage when he was born. Pete Bancini continually declares that he is tired, and at one point he tells the other patients that he was born dead.

Martini Another hospital patient. Martini lives in a world of delusional hallucinations, but McMurphy includes him in the board and card games with the other patients.

Old Blastic A patient who is a vegetable. Bromden has a prophetic dream about a mechanical slaughterhouse in which Old Blastic is murdered. He wakes up to discover that Old Blastic died in the night.

Ellis A patient who was once an Acute. Ellis's excessive electroshock therapy transformed him into a Chronic. In the daytime, he is nailed to the wall. He frequently urinates on himself.

The lifeguard A patient and a former football player. The lifeguard was committed to the ward eight years ago. He often experiences hallucinations. The lifeguard reveals a key fact to McMurphy—that committed patients can leave only when Nurse Ratched permits—which changes McMurphy's initial rebelliousness into temporary conformity.

Sandy Gilfillian A prostitute who knows McMurphy.

Ruckly A Chronic patient. Ruckly, like Ellis, was once an Acute, but was transformed into a Chronic due to a botched lobotomy.

Scanlon The only Acute besides McMurphy who was involuntarily committed to the hospital. Scanlon has fantasies of blowing things up.

Sefelt and Frederickson Epileptic patients. Sefelt hates to take his medications because they make his teeth fall out, so he gives them to Frederickson, who likes to take Sefelt's dose in addition to his own. Although Sefelt and Frederickson require more medical care than some of the other nonmedicated patients, they still do not receive much care or attention by the staff, who are much more concerned with making the disorderly patients orderly.

Mr. Turkle The black nighttime orderly for Nurse Ratched's ward. Mr. Turkle is kind to Bromden, untying the sheets that confine him to his bed at night, and he goes along with the nighttime ward party.

Maxwell Taber A former patient who stayed in Nurse Ratched's ward before McMurphy arrived. When Maxwell Taber questioned the nurse's authority, she punished him with electroshock therapy. After the treatments made him completely docile, he was allowed to leave the hospital. He is considered a successful cure by the hospital staff.

Chief Tee Ah Millatoona Chief Bromden's father, also known as The Pine That Stands Tallest on the Mountain, is chief of the Columbia Indians. He married a Caucasian woman and took her last name. She made him feel small and drove him to alcoholism. The chief's marriage and submission to a white woman makes an important statement about the oppression of the natural order by modern society and also reflects white society's encroachment on Native Americans.

Public Relation A fat, bald bureaucrat who wears a girdle. Public Relation leads tours of the ward, pointing out that it is nice and pleasant.

Nurse Pilbow A strict Catholic with a prominent birthmark on her face that she attempts to scrub away. Nurse Pilbow is afraid of the patients' sexuality.

Rawler   A patient on the Disturbed ward. Rawler commits suicide by cutting off his testicles. This actual castration symbolizes the psychological emasculation to which the patients are routinely subjected.

CHARACTER LIST

ANALYSIS OF MAJOR CHARACTERS

CHIEF BROMDEN

Chief Bromden, nicknamed "Chief Broom" because the aides make him sweep the halls, narrates *One Flew Over the Cuckoo's Nest*. Although he says that he is telling the story about "the hospital, and her, and the guys—and about McMurphy," he is also telling the story of his own journey toward sanity. When the novel begins, Bromden is paranoid, bullied, and surrounded much of the time by a hallucinated fog that represents both his medicated state and his desire to hide from reality. Moreover, he believes that he is extremely weak, even though he used to be immensely strong; because he believes it, he *is* extremely weak. By the end of the novel, the fog has cleared, and Bromden has recovered the personal strength to euthanize McMurphy, escape from the hospital, and record his account of the events.

Bromden is six feet seven inches tall, but because he has been belittled for so long, he thinks he "used to be big, but not no more." He has been a patient in an Oregon psychiatric hospital for ten years. Everyone in the hospital believes that he is deaf and dumb. When McMurphy begins to pull him out of the fog, he realizes the source of his charade: "it wasn't me that started acting deaf; it was people that first started acting like I was too dumb to hear or see or say anything at all." As Bromden himself is demystified, so too is the truth behind what has oppressed him and hindered his recovery.

This oppression has been in place since Bromden's childhood. He is the son of Chief Tee Ah Millatoona, which means The Pine That Stands Tallest on the Mountain, and a white woman, Mary Louise Bromden, the dominant force in the couple. Chief Bromden bears his mother's last name; his father's acceptance of her name symbolizes her dominance over him. In one telling experience, when Bromden was ten years old, three government officials came to see his father about buying the tribe's land so they could build a hydroelectric dam, but Bromden was home alone. When he tried to speak to the officials, they acted as if he was not there. This experience sows the seeds for his withdrawal into himself, and initiates the out-side world's treatment of him as if he were deaf and dumb. Bro-mden's mother joined forces with some of the members of the tribe to pressure Bromden's father to sell the land. Bromden, like his father, is a big man who comes to feel small and helpless.

The reason for Bromden's hospitalization is cloaked in ambigu-ity. He may have had a breakdown from witnessing the decline of his father or from the horrors of fighting in World War II. Both of these possible scenarios involve an emasculating and controlling authority—in the first case the government officials, in the second the army. These authority figures provide Bromden with fodder for his dark vision of society as an oppressive conglomeration that he calls the Combine. It is also possible that, like McMurphy, Bromden was sane when he entered the hospital but that his sanity slipped when he received what is rumored to be 200 electroshock treat-ments. The paranoia and hallucinations he suffers from, which cen-ter on hidden machines in the hospital that physically and psychologically control the patients, can be read as metaphors for the dehumanization he has experienced in his life.

RANDLE MCMURPHY

Randle McMurphy—big, loud, sexual, dirty, and confident—is an obvious foil for the quiet and repressed Bromden and the sterile and mechanical Nurse Ratched. His loud, free laughter stuns the other patients, who have grown accustomed to repressed emotions. Throughout the entire moment of his introduction, not a single voice rises to meet his.

McMurphy represents sexuality, freedom, and self-determina-tion—characteristics that clash with the oppressed ward, which is controlled by Nurse Ratched. Through Chief Bromden's narration, the novel establishes that McMurphy is not, in fact, crazy, but rather that he is trying to manipulate the system to his advantage. His belief that the hospital would be more comfortable than the Pendleton Work Farm, where he was serving a six-month sentence, haunts McMurphy later when he discovers the power Nurse Ratched wields over him—that she can send him for electroshock treatments and keep him committed as long as she likes. McMurphy's sanity contrasts with what Kesey implies is an insane institution.

Whether insane or not, the hospital is undeniably in control of the fates of its patients. McMurphy's fate as the noncomforming insurrectionist is foreshadowed by the fate of Maxwell Taber, a former patient who was also, according to Nurse Ratched, a manipulator. Taber was subjected to electroshock treatments and possibly brain work, which leaves him docile and unable to think. When Ratched equates McMurphy with Taber, we get an inkling of McMurphy's prospects. McMurphy's trajectory through the novel is the opposite of Bromden's: he starts out sane and powerful but ends up a helpless vegetable, having sacrificed himself for the benefit of all the patients.

McMurphy's self-sacrifice on behalf of his ward-mates echoes Christ's sacrifice of himself on the cross to redeem humankind. McMurphy's actions frequently parallel Christ's actions in the Gospels. McMurphy undergoes a kind of baptism upon entering the ward, and he slowly gathers disciples around him as he increases his rebellion against Ratched. When he takes the group of patients fishing, he is like Christ leading his twelve disciples to the sea to test their faith. Finally, McMurphy's ultimate sacrifice, his attack on Ratched, combined with the symbolism of the cross-shaped electroshock table and McMurphy's request for "a crown of thorns," cements the image of the Christ-like martyrdom that McMurphy has achieved by sacrificing his freedom and sanity.

NURSE RATCHED

A former army nurse, Nurse Ratched represents the oppressive mechanization, dehumanization, and emasculation of modern society—in Bromden's words, the Combine. Her nickname is "Big Nurse," which sounds like Big Brother, the name used in George Orwell's novel *1984* to refer to an oppressive and all-knowing authority. Bromden describes Ratched as being like a machine, and her behavior fits this description: even her name is reminiscent of a mechanical tool, sounding like both "ratchet" and "wretched." She enters the novel, and the ward, "with a gust of cold." Ratched has complete control over every aspect of the ward, as well as almost complete control over her own emotions. In the first few pages we see her show her "hideous self" to Bromden and the aides, only to regain her doll-like composure before any of the patients catch a glimpse. Her ability to present a false self suggests that the mechanistic and oppressive forces in society gain ascendance through the dishonesty of the powerful. Without being aware of the oppression, the quiet and docile slowly become weakened and gradually are subsumed.

Nurse Ratched does possess a nonmechanical and undeniably human feature in her large bosom, which she conceals as best she can beneath a heavily starched uniform. Her large breasts both exude sexuality and emphasize her role as a twisted mother figure for the ward. She is able to act like "an angel of mercy" while at the same time shaming the patients into submission; she knows their weak spots and exactly where to peck. The patients try to please her during the Group Meetings by airing their dirtiest, darkest secrets, and then they feel deeply ashamed for how she made them act, even though they have done nothing. She maintains her power by the strategic use of shame and guilt, as well as by a determination to "divide and conquer" her patients.

McMurphy manages to ruffle Ratched because he plays her game: he picks up on her weak spots right away. He uses his overt sexuality to throw her off her machinelike track, and he is not taken in by her thin facade of compassion or her falsely therapeutic tactics. When McMurphy rips her shirt open at the end of the novel, he symbolically exposes her hypocrisy and deceit, and she is never able to regain power.

THEMES, MOTIFS & SYMBOLS

THEMES

Themes are the fundamental and often universal ideas explored in a literary work.

WOMEN AS CASTRATORS

With the exception of the prostitutes, who are portrayed as good, the women in *One Flew Over the Cuckoo's Nest* are uniformly threatening and terrifying figures. Bromden, the narrator, and McMurphy, the protagonist, both tend to describe the suffering of the mental patients as a matter of emasculation or castration at the hands of Nurse Ratched and the hospital supervisor, who is also a woman. The fear of women is one of the novel's most central features. The male characters seem to agree with Harding, who complains, "We are victims of a matriarchy here."

Indeed, most of the male patients have been damaged by relationships with overpowering women. For instance, Bromden's mother is portrayed as a castrating woman; her husband took her last name, and she turned a big, strong chief into a small, weak alcoholic. According to Bromden, she built herself up emotionally, becoming bigger than either he or his father, by constantly putting them down. Similarly, Billy Bibbit's mother treats him like an infant and does not allow him to develop sexually. Through sex with Candy, Billy briefly regains his confidence. It is no coincidence that this act, which symbolically resurrects his manhood, also literally introduces his penis to sexual activity. Thus, his manhood—in both senses—returns until Ratched takes it away by threatening to tell his mother and driving him to commit suicide.

More explicit images of and references to castration appear later in the novel, cementing Kesey's idea of emasculation by the frigid nurse. When Rawler, a patient in the Disturbed ward, commits suicide by cutting off his own testicles, Bromden remarks that "all the guy had to do was wait," implying that the institution itself would have castrated him in the long run. The hospital, run by women, treats only male patients, showing how women have the ability to emasculate even the most masculine of men. Finally, near the end of the novel, after McMurphy has already received three shock treatments that do not seem to have had an effect on him, Nurse Ratched suggests taking more drastic measures: "an operation." She means, of course, a lobotomy, but McMurphy beats her to the punch by joking about castration. Both operations remove a man's individuality, freedom, and ability for sexual expression. Kesey portrays the two operations as symbolically the same.

SOCIETY'S DESTRUCTION OF NATURAL IMPULSES

Kesey uses mechanical imagery to represent modern society and biological imagery to represent nature. By means of mechanisms and machines, society gains control of and suppresses individuality and natural impulses. The hospital, representative of society at large, is decidedly unnatural: the aides and Nurse Ratched are described as being made of motley machine parts. In Chief Bromden's dream, when Blastic is disemboweled, rust, not blood, spills out, revealing that the hospital destroyed not only his life but his humanity as well. Bromden's realization that the hospital treats human beings in an unnatural fashion, and his concomitant growing self-awareness, occur as a surrounding fog dissipates. It is no surprise that Bromden believes this fog is a construction of machines controlled by the hospital and by Nurse Ratched.

Bromden, as the son of an Indian chief, is a combination of pure, natural individuality and a spirit almost completely subverted by mechanized society. Early on, he had free will, and he can remember and describe going hunting in the woods with his relatives and the way they spear salmon. The government, however, eventually succeeds in paying off the tribe so their fishing area can be converted into a profitable hydroelectric dam. The tribe members are banished into the technological workforce, where they become "hypnotized by routine," like the "half-life things" that Bromden witnesses coming out of the train while he is on fishing excursions. In the novel's present time, Bromden himself ends up semi-catatonic and paranoid, a mechanical drone who is still able to think and conjecture to some extent on his own.

McMurphy represents unbridled individuality and free expression—both intellectual and sexual. One idea presented in this novel is that a man's virility is equated with a state of nature, and the state of civilized society requires that he be desexualized. But McMurphy battles against letting the oppressive society make him into a machinelike drone, and he manages to maintain his individuality until his ultimate objective—bringing this individuality to the others—is complete. However, when his wildness is provoked one too many times by Nurse Ratched, he ends up being destroyed by modern society's machines of oppression.

THE IMPORTANCE OF EXPRESSING SEXUALITY

It is implied throughout the novel that a healthy expression of sexuality is a key component of sanity, and that repression of sexuality leads directly to insanity. Most of the patients have warped sexual identities because of damaging relationships with women. Perverted sexual expressions are said to take place in the ward: the aides supposedly engage in illicit "sex acts" that nobody witnesses, and on several occasions it is suggested that they rape patients, such as Taber, with Ratched's implicit permission, symbolized by the jar of Vaseline she leaves with them. Add to that the castrating power of Nurse Ratched, and the ward is left with, as Harding says, "comical little creatures who can't even achieve masculinity in the rabbit world." Missing from the halls of the mental hospital are healthy, natural expressions of sexuality between two people.

McMurphy's bold assertion of his sexuality, symbolized from the start by his playing cards depicting fifty-two sexual positions, his pride in having had a voracious fifteen-year-old lover, and his Moby-Dick boxer shorts, clashes with the sterile and sexless ward that Nurse Ratched tries to maintain. We learn that McMurphy first had sex at age ten with a girl perhaps even younger, and that her dress from that momentous occasion, which inspired him to become a "dedicated lover," still hangs outdoors for everyone to see. McMurphy's refusal to conform to society mirrors his refusal to desexualize himself, and the sexuality exuding from his personality is like a dress waving in the wind like a flag.

McMurphy attempts to cure Billy Bibbit of his stutter by arranging for him to lose his virginity with Candy. Instead, Billy gets shamed into suicide by the puritanical Ratched. By the end of the novel, McMurphy has been beaten into the ground to the point that he resorts to sexual violence—which had never been a part of his persona previous to being committed, despite Nurse Pilbow's fears—by ripping open Ratched's uniform.

FALSE DIAGNOSES OF INSANITY

McMurphy's sanity, symbolized by his free laughter, open sexuality, strength, size, and confidence, stands in contrast to what Kesey implies, ironically and tragically, is an insane institution. Nurse Ratched tells another nurse that McMurphy seems to be a manipulator, just like a former patient, Maxwell Taber. Taber, Bromden explains, was a "big, griping Acute" who once asked a nurse what kind of medication he was being given. He was subjected to electroshock treatments and possibly brain work, which left him docile and unable to think. The insanity of the institution is foregrounded when a man who asks a simple question is tortured and rendered inhuman. It is a Catch-22: only a sane man would question an irrational system, but the act of questioning means his sanity will inevitably be compromised.

Throughout the novel, the sane actions of men contrast with the insane actions of the institution. At the end of Part II, when McMurphy and the patients stage a protest against Nurse Ratched for not letting them watch the World Series, a sensible request for which McMurphy generates a sensible solution, she loses control and, as Bromden notes, looks as crazy as they do. Moreover, Kesey encourages the reader to consider the value of alternative states of perception, which some people also might consider crazy. For instance, Bromden's hallucinations about hidden machinery may seem crazy, but in actuality they reveal his insight into the hospital's insidious power over the patients.

In addition, when the patients go on the fishing excursion they discover that mental illness can have an aspect of power in that they can intimidate the station attendants with their insanity. Harding gives Hitler as an example in discussing Ratched, suggesting that she, like Hitler, is a psychopath who has discovered how to use her insanity to her advantage. Bromden, at one point, thinks to himself, "You're making sense, old man, a sense of your own. You're not crazy the way they think." "[C]razy the way they think," however, is all that matters in this hospital. The authority figures decide who is sane and who is insane, and by deciding it, they make it reality.

MOTIFS

Motifs are recurring structures, contrasts, or literary devices that can help to develop and inform the text's major themes.

INVISIBILITY

Many important elements in the novel are either hidden from view or invisible. For example, Bromden tries to be as invisible as possible. He has achieved this invisibility by pretending not to understand what is going on around him, so people notice him less and less. Moreover, he imagines a fog surrounding him that hides him and keeps him safe. He keeps both his body and his mind hidden.

Bromden's hallucinations about hidden machines that control the patients call attention to the fact that the power over the patients is usually covert. He imagines that the patients are implanted with tiny machines that record and control their movements from the inside. The truth is that Nurse Ratched manages to rule by insinuation, without ever having to be explicit about her accusations and threats, so it seems as though the patients themselves have absorbed her influence—she becomes a sort of twisted conscience.

When McMurphy smashes through the glass window of the Nurses' Station, his excuse is that the glass was so clean he could not see it. By smashing it, he reminds the patients that although they cannot always see Ratched's or society's manipulation, it still operates on them.

THE POWER OF LAUGHTER

The power of laughter resonates throughout the novel. McMurphy's laughter is the first genuine laughter heard on the ward in years. McMurphy's first inkling that things are strange among the patients is that none of them are able to laugh; they can only smile and snicker behind their hands. Bromden remembers a scene from his childhood when his father and relatives mocked some government officials, and he realizes how powerful their laughter was: "I forget sometimes what laughter can do." For McMurphy, laughter is a potent defense against society's insanity, and anyone who cannot laugh properly has no chance of surviving. By the end of the fishing trip, Harding, Scanlon, Doctor Spivey, and Sefelt are all finally able to participate in real, thunderous laughter, a sign of their physical and psychological recovery.

REAL VERSUS IMAGINED SIZE

Bromden describes people by their true size, not merely their physical size. Kesey implies that when people allow others, such as governments and institutions, to define their worth, they can end up far from their natural state. Nurse Ratched's true size, for example, is "big as a tractor," because she is powerful and unstoppable. Bromden, though he is six feet seven inches tall, feels much smaller and weaker. He tells McMurphy, "I used to be big, but not no more." As for McMurphy, Bromden says he is "broad as Papa was tall," and his father was named The Pine That Stands Tallest on the Mountain. Bromden says his mother was twice the size of he and his father put together, because she belittled them both so much. With McMurphy's help, Bromden is gradually "blown back up to full size" as he regains his self-esteem, sexuality, and individuality.

SYMBOLS

Symbols are objects, characters, figures, or colors used to represent abstract ideas or concepts.

THE FOG MACHINE

Fog is a phenomenon that clouds our vision of the world. In this novel, fogs symbolize a lack of insight and an escape from reality. When Bromden starts to slip away from reality, because of his medication or out of fear, he hallucinates fog drifting into the ward. He imagines that there are hidden fog machines in the vents and that they are controlled by the staff. Although it can be frightening at times, Bromden considers the fog to be a safe place; he can hide in it and ignore reality. Beyond what it means for Bromden, the fog represents the state of mind that Ratched imposes on the patients with her strict, mind-numbing routines and humiliating treatment. When McMurphy arrives, he drags all the patients out of the fog.

MCMURPHY'S BOXER SHORTS

McMurphy's boxer shorts are black satin with a pattern of white whales with red eyes. A literature major gave them to him, saying that McMurphy is himself a symbol. The shorts, of course, are also highly symbolic. First, the white whales call to mind Moby-Dick, one of the most potent symbols in American literature. One common interpretation of Moby-Dick is that the whale is a phallic symbol, which obviously suggests McMurphy's blatant sexuality—the little white whales cover McMurphy's underwear, which he gleefully reveals to Nurse Ratched. Moby-Dick also represents the pervasive evil that inspires Ahab's obsessive, futile pursuit. Here, the implication is that McMurphy is to Moby-Dick as Ratched is to Ahab. A third interpretation is that Moby-Dick stands for the power of nature, signifying McMurphy's untamed nature that conflicts with the controlled institution. Lastly, in Melville's novel Moby-Dick is associated with God, which resonates with McMurphy's role as a Christ figure. Finally, the whale boxer shorts poke fun at academia and its elaborate interpretations of symbols.

THE ELECTROSHOCK THERAPY TABLE

The electroshock therapy table is explicitly associated with crucifixion. It is shaped like a cross, with straps across the wrists and over the head. Moreover, the table performs a function similar to the public crucifixions of Roman times. Ellis, Ruckly, and Taber—Acutes whose lives were destroyed by electroshock therapy—serve as public examples of what happens to those who rebel against the ruling powers. Ellis makes the reference explicit: he is actually nailed to the wall. This foreshadows that McMurphy, who is associated with Christ images, will be sacrificed.

SYMBOLS

SUMMARY & ANALYSIS

PART I

From the beginning of the novel to McMurphy's bet with the patients

SUMMARY

> It's still hard for me to have a clear mind thinking on it. But it's the truth even if it didn't happen.
> (See QUOTATIONS, p. 47)

Chief Bromden, a long-term patient in Nurse Ratched's psychiatric ward, narrates the events of the novel. The book begins as he awakens to a typical day on the ward, feeling paranoid about the illicit nighttime activities of the ward's three black aides. The aides mock him for being a pushover, even though he is six feet seven inches tall, and they make him sweep the hallways for them, nicknaming him "Chief Broom." Bromden is half Indian and pretends to be deaf and dumb; as a result, he overhears all the secrets on the ward and is barely noticed by anyone despite his stature.

Nurse Ratched, whom Bromden refers to as "the Big Nurse," enters the ward with a gust of cold air. Bromden describes Ratched as having "skin like flesh-colored enamel" and lips and fingertips the strange orange color of polished steel. Her one feminine feature is her oversized bosom, which she tries to conceal beneath a starched white uniform. When she gets angry with the aides, Bromden sees her get "big as a tractor." She orders the aides to shave Bromden, and he begins to scream and hallucinate that he is being surrounded by machine-made fog until he is forcedly medicated. He tells us that his forthcoming story about the hospital might seem "too awful to be the truth."

Bromden regains consciousness in the day room. Here, he tells us that a public relations man sometimes leads tours around the ward, pointing out the cheery atmosphere and claiming that the ward is run without the brutality exercised in previous generations. Today, the ward's monotony is interrupted when Randle McMurphy, a new patient, arrives. McMurphy's appearance is preceded by his boisterous, brassy voice and his confident, iron-heeled walk. McMurphy laughs when the patients are stunned silent by his entrance. It is the first real laugh that the ward has heard in years.

McMurphy, a large redhead with a devilish grin, swaggers around the ward in his motorcycle cap and dirty work-farm clothes, with a leather jacket over one arm. He introduces himself as a gambling fool, saying that he requested to be transferred to the hospital to escape the drudgery of the Pendleton Work Farm. He asks to meet the "bull goose looney" so he can take over as the man in charge. He encounters Billy Bibbit, a thirty-one-year-old baby-faced man with a severe stutter, and Dale Harding, the effeminate and educated president of the Patients' Council. All the while, McMurphy sidesteps the attempts of the daytime aides to herd him into the admission routine of a shower, an injection, and a rectal thermometer.

McMurphy surveys the day room. The patients are divided into two main categories: the Acutes, who are considered curable, and the Chronics, whom Bromden, himself a Chronic, calls "machines with flaws inside that can't be repaired." The Chronics who can move around are Walkers, and the rest are either Wheelers or Vegetables. Some Chronics are patients who arrived at the hospital as Acutes but were mentally crippled by excessive shock treatment or brain surgery, common practices in the hospital. Nurse Ratched encourages the Acutes to spy on one another. If one reveals an embarrassing or incriminating personal detail, the rest race to write it in the logbook. Their reward for such disclosures is sleeping late the next morning.

Nurse Ratched runs her ward on a strict schedule, controlling every movement with absolute precision. The nurse has selected her aides for their inherent cruelty and her staff for their submissiveness. Bromden recalls Maxwell Taber, a patient who demanded information about his medications. He was sent for multiple electroshock treatments and rendered completely docile. Eventually, he was considered cured and was discharged. Bromden conceives of society as a huge, oppressive conglomeration that he calls the Combine, and he sees the hospital as a factory for "fixing up mistakes made in the neighborhoods and in the schools and in the churches."

During the Group Meeting, Nurse Ratched reopens the topic of Harding's difficult relationship with his wife. When McMurphy makes lewd jokes at the nurse's expense, she retaliates by reading his file aloud, focusing on his arrest for statutory rape. McMurphy regales the group with stories about the sexual appetite of his fif-teen-year-old lover. Even Doctor Spivey enjoys McMurphy's humorous rebellion against Ratched. The doctor reads from the file, "Don't overlook the possibility that this man might be feigning psy-chosis to escape the drudgery of the work farm," to which McMur-phy responds, "Doctor, do I look like a sane man?" McMurphy has similar defiant retorts for almost any action Ratched can consider, which perturbs Ratched greatly. McMurphy is disconcerted that the patients and the doctor can smile but not laugh. Bromden remem-bers a meeting that was broken up when Pete Bancini, a lifelong Chronic who constantly declared he was tired, became lucid for a moment and hit one of the aides with a heavy iron ball. The nurse injected him with a sedative as he had a nervous breakdown.

During the meeting, the patients tear into Harding's sexual prob-lems. Afterward, they are embarrassed, as always, at their vicious-ness. As a new participant and observer, McMurphy tells Harding that the meeting was a "pecking party"—the men acted like a bunch of chickens pecking at another chicken's wound. He warns them that a pecking party can wipe out the whole flock. When McMur-phy points out that Nurse Ratched pecks first, Harding becomes defensive and states that Ratched's procedure is therapeutic. McMurphy replies that she is merely a "ball-cutter."

Harding finally agrees that Ratched is a cruel, vicious woman. He explains that everyone in the ward is a rabbit in a world ruled by wolves. They are in the hospital because they are unable to accept their roles as rabbits. Nurse Ratched is one of the wolves, and she is there to train them to accept their rabbit roles. She can make a patient shrink with shame and fear while acting like a concerned angel of mercy. Ratched never accuses directly, but she rules others through insinuation. McMurphy says that they should tell her to go to hell with her insinuating questions. Harding warns that such hos-tile behavior will earn a man electroshock therapy and a stay in the Disturbed ward. He points to Bromden, calling him "a six-foot-eight sweeping machine" as a result of all the shock treatment he has received. Harding asserts that the only power men have over women is sexual violence, but they cannot even exercise that power against the icy, impregnable nurse. McMurphy makes a bet with the other patients that he can make Nurse Ratched lose her temper within a week. He explains that he conned his way out of the work farm by feigning insanity, and Nurse Ratched is unprepared for an enemy with a "trigger-quick mind" like his.

ANALYSIS

Chief Bromden, the narrator of *One Flew Over the Cuckoo's Nest,* is a complex character whose own story is revealed as he tells the story of the ward at large. Because he feigns deafness, he is privy to information that is kept from the other patients. In this way, he is a more informed narrator than any other patient. However, Bromden's reliability as a narrator is unclear because we constantly see reminders of his psychological disorder. The main indications of his illness are paranoia and frequent hallucinations. His paranoia is often justified, as the patients are indeed treated barbarically. But his hallucinations, though they seem crazy at first, metaphorically reveal his deep, intuitive understanding of his surroundings. For example, the fog machine he hallucinates represents his state of mind—he is overmedicated or simply too fearful to face the stark reality beyond the fog. The fog machine also represents the power-lessness of the patients, who are encouraged and sometimes forced by the staff to stay hidden in their own individual fogs.

Bromden sees modern society as a machinelike, oppressive force, and the hospital as a repair shop for the people who do not fit into their role as cogs in the machine. Bromden's way of inter-preting the world emphasizes the oppressive social pressure to con-form: those who do not conform to society's rules and conventions are considered defective products and are labeled mentally ill and sent for treatment. Thus, the mental hospital is a metaphor for the oppression Kesey sees in modern society, preceding the emergence of the 1960s counterculture. A hospital, normally a place where the ill go to be cured, becomes a dangerous place; Ellis, Ruckly, and Taber, for instance, are electroshocked until they become doc-ile or even vegetables. The hospital is not about healing, but about dehumanizing and manipulating the patients until they are weak and willing to conform.

At the center of this controlled universe is Nurse Ratched, a rep-resentative of what Bromden calls the Combine, meaning the oppressive force of society and authority. Bromden describes her in mechanical, inhuman terms. She tries to conceal her large breasts as much as possible, and her face is like that of a doll, with a subtle edge of cruelty. Bromden imagines that the hospital is full of hidden machinery—wires, magnets, and more sinister contraptions—used by Nurse Ratched to control the patients. The nurse is, in fact, in complete control of the ward, and the tools she uses—psychological intimidation, divide-and-conquer techniques, and physical abuse—

are every bit as powerful and insidious as the hidden machinery Bromden imagines.

Immediately upon his arrival, McMurphy challenges the ward with his exuberant vitality and sexuality, which are directly opposed to the sterile, mechanical nature of the hospital and modern society. He is set up as an obvious foil to Nurse Ratched, as well as to the silent and repressed Bromden. McMurphy's discussion with Harding reveals the misogynistic undertones of *One Flew Over the Cuckoo's Nest*. The patients associate matriarchy with castration, explaining the lifelessness and oppressiveness of modern society as a product of female dominance.

PART I, CONTINUED

From Bromden's description of the speeding clock to the end of Part I

SUMMARY

Bromden believes that Nurse Ratched can set the clock to any speed. Sometimes everything is painfully fast and sometimes painfully slow. His only escape is being in the fog where time does not exist. He notes that whoever controls the fog machine has not turned it on as much since McMurphy's arrival. Later, Bromden explains his captivation with McMurphy's con-artistry, which he displays while playing cards with the other patients. McMurphy wins hundreds of cigarettes and then allows his opponents to win them back. That night, McMurphy whispers to Bromden and implies that he knows he is not really deaf. Bromden does not take his night medication and has a nightmare that the hospital is a mechanical slaughterhouse. The staff hangs Old Blastic on a meat hook and slashes him open, and ash and rust pour out of the wound. Mr. Turkle wakes him from the nightmare.

Everyone wakes to McMurphy's boisterous singing in the latrine. When Williams, one of the aides, will not let him have toothpaste before the appointed time, McMurphy brushes his teeth with soap. Bromden hides his smile, as he is reminded of how his father also used to win confrontations with humor. Ratched prepares to reprimand McMurphy for his singing, but he stops her cold by stepping out of the bathroom wearing only a towel. He says that someone has taken his clothes, so he has nothing to wear. Ratched furiously reprimands the aides for failing to issue a patient's outfit to McMurphy. When Washington, another aide, offers McMurphy an outfit, McMurphy drops the towel to take it, revealing that all along he was wearing a pair of boxer shorts—black satin covered with white whales. Ratched manages to regain her composure with serious effort.

McMurphy is even more confident that morning. He asks Ratched to turn down the recorded music playing in the ward. She politely refuses, explaining that some of the Chronics are hard of hearing and cannot entertain themselves without the music turned up loudly. She also refuses to allow them to play cards in another room, citing a lack of staff to supervise two rooms. Doctor Spivey comes to get McMurphy for an interview, and they return talking and laughing together. At the Group Meeting, the doctor announces McMurphy's plan for the radio to be played at a higher volume, so that the hard-of-hearing patients can enjoy it more. He proposes that the other patients go to another room to read or play cards. Since the Chronics are easy to supervise, the staff can be split between the rooms. Ratched restrains herself from losing her temper.

McMurphy starts a Monopoly game with Cheswick, Martini, and Harding that goes on for three days. McMurphy makes sure he does not lose his temper with any of the staff. Once, he does get angry with the patients for being "too chicken-shit." He then requests that Ratched allow them to watch the World Series, even though it is not the regulation TV time. In order to make up for this, he proposes that they do the cleaning chores at night and watch the TV in the afternoon, but Ratched refuses to change the schedule. He proposes a vote at the Group Meeting, but only Cheswick is brave enough—or crazy enough—to defy Ratched, since the others are afraid of long-term repercussions. McMurphy, furious, says he is going to escape, and Fredrickson goads him into showing them how he would do it. McMurphy bets them that he can lift the cement control panel in the tub room and use it to break through the reinforced windows. Everybody knows it will be impossible to lift the massive panel, but he makes such a sincere effort that for one moment they all believe it is possible.

Bromden remembers how at the old hospital they did not have pictures on the wall or television. He recalls Public Relations saying, "A man that would want to run away from a place as nice as this, why, there'd be something wrong with him." Bromden senses that the fog machine has been turned on again. He explains how the fog makes him feel safe and that McMurphy keeps trying to drag them out of the fog where they will be "easy to get at." He then overhears someone talking about Old Rawler, a patient in the Disturbed unit who killed himself by cutting off his testicles. Bromden then further describes getting lost in the fog and finding himself two or three times a month at the electroshock room.

At the next Group Meeting, Bromden feels immersed in fog and cannot follow the group as they grill Billy about his stutter and failed relationship with a girl. McMurphy proposes another vote regarding the TV, with the support of some of the other patients. It is the first day of the World Series. Bromden observes the hands go up as McMurphy drags all twenty Acutes out of the fog. Ratched declares the proposal defeated, however, because none of the twenty Chronics raised their hands and McMurphy needs a majority. McMurphy finally persuades Bromden to raise his hand, but Ratched says the vote is closed. During the afternoon cleaning chores, McMurphy declares that it is time for the game. When he turns on the TV, Ratched cuts its power, but McMurphy does not budge from the armchair. The Acutes follow suit and sit in front of the blank TV. She screams and rants at them for breaking the schedule, and McMurphy wins his bet that he could make her lose her composure.

ANALYSIS

Bromden's reliability as a narrator becomes clear as we realize how incredibly observant he is. Unlike the other patients, Bromden notices how carefully McMurphy sets them up to lose their cigarettes. Moreover, Bromden's bizarre dream about Old Blastic turns out to be prophetic, demonstrating that his altered states of perception are significant rather than simply crazy. Bromden perceives the hospital not as a place promoting health but as a mechanized slaughterhouse where not only humans, but also humanity, is murdered. Old Blastic is hung on a meat hook and disemboweled, but rust and ash pour from his wound rather than flesh and blood. Bromden's dreams metaphorically reveal his profound insight into the dehumanizing and mechanizing forces of the hospital.

Bromden's hallucination that he is surrounded by fog extends to the other patients—he thinks that they are lost in fog too. This is clearly a delusion, but metaphorically it is true. The status quo enforced by Nurse Ratched functions to dull the patients' senses.

Her tight routine makes everything seem to move either too slow or too fast. The too-loud music makes conversation difficult and frustrating. In response to the ever-extending fog, or a clouding of one's unique thoughts and needs, Bromden describes McMurphy's actions as dragging the patients out of the fog. By resisting Ratched, McMurphy awakens the patients to their own ability to resist her, and thereby helps them see beyond the fog. Bromden at first does not attribute his rebellious vote to his own willpower, but rather to some mysterious power on McMurphy's part. Then he later realizes, "No. That's not the truth. I lifted [my hand] myself." Bromden is very slowly beginning to see himself as an individual with free will; his recognition that the fog blankets the entire ward is an ironic indication that his own fog is beginning to lift.

McMurphy's small but continual infractions of the rules are assertions of his own individuality. McMurphy's defiance encourages the other patients to defy Ratched by gambling for cigarettes. He succeeds in drawing the other patients into rebellion against Ratched's authority, because she forbids gambling for anything but matches. Furthermore, the incident with the towel reflects McMurphy's faith in humor as a means to resist Ratched's authority. Earlier, when McMurphy suggests that the patients laugh at Ratched, Harding scoffs at the idea. Harding asserts that the only effective tool of resistance against Ratched is the penis, the instrument of male violence against dominant femininity. Although McMurphy's resistance to Ratched's authority does include a sexual element, McMurphy combines sexuality with humor, not violence. The symbolism of the encounter is heightened by McMurphy's boxers, a gift from a college student who said that McMurphy was himself a literary symbol. White whales evoke the famous Moby Dick, a beast associated in Herman Melville's novel *Moby-Dick* with a variety of symbolic meanings, including masculinity, unseen power, insanity, and freedom. When McMurphy flaunts these symbolic boxers before Nurse Ratched, he is connected to each of these interpretations, reminding the reader that he serves as a prominent symbol within the novel.

McMurphy's display of his whale boxer shorts affirms his belief that men should not be ashamed of their sexuality, whereas making the patients ashamed of their sexuality is one of Ratched's major ways of dominating them. Ratched's strategy is evident in her treatment of Billy Bibbit, a thirty-one-year-old virgin dominated into celibacy by his mother. Though it is obvious to us that Billy needs to find a way out from under his mother's shadow, Ratched does the opposite of helping him do this, defining his sexuality in terms of inadequacy and shame. Rather than attempting to cure the patients of their problems, Ratched increases their discomfort as a way of building her own power.

McMurphy's personal rebellion against Ratched's authority expands and becomes the patients' collective rebellion, with McMurphy as their unofficial leader. When McMurphy wins his bet, he does so with the other patients' help as they all join him in protest. Meanwhile, Bromden's perceptions of the situation develop and change. When Ratched begins screaming hysterically, Bromden states that anyone who walked into the room at the moment would think they were all crazy. Insanity is no longer a characteristic of the patients alone. Before, Bromden saw the patients as defective. Now, with the help of a unified force against the mechanistic Combine, he is beginning to see the established order as defective as well.

PART II

SUMMARY

The tables are turned in the ward as everyone watches Ratched in the glassed-in Nurses' Station after her outburst. She cannot escape the patients' stares, just as they can never escape hers. Ratched strains to regain composure for the staff meeting she called. Bromden says the fog is completely gone now. He always cleans the staff room during meetings, but after his vote, he fears that everyone will realize that he is not really deaf. He goes anyway, knowing that Ratched is suspicious of him. Doctor Spivey attempts to get the meeting started while Ratched uses silence to assert her power. The staff, misreading Ratched's silence as approval, decides that McMurphy is potentially violent and should be sent to the Disturbed ward. Ratched disagrees; she declares instead that McMurphy is an ordinary man, subject to the same fears and timidity as the others. Since McMurphy is committed, Ratched knows she can control how long he spends in the hospital, and she decides to take her time with him.

Ratched assigns McMurphy the chore of cleaning the latrines, but he continues to nettle her in every way possible. Bromden marvels that the Combine has not broken him. One night, he wakes up and looks out the window and gazes in wonder at the countryside. Bromden observes a dog sniffing around the building and a flock of geese flying overhead. He watches as the dog runs toward the highway, where the headlights of an oncoming car are visible. During the Group Meetings, the patients begin to air their long-silent complaints about the rules.

The ward is taken to the hospital's pool to swim. McMurphy learns from the patient serving as the lifeguard that someone who is committed to the hospital is released only at the discretion of the staff. McMurphy had believed he could leave as soon as he served the time remaining on his work farm sentence. Cowed by his new knowledge, he behaves more conservatively around Ratched. During the next Group Meeting, Cheswick brings up the problem of cigarette rationing, but McMurphy does not support him. Ratched sends Cheswick to Disturbed for a while. After he returns, on the way to the pool, Cheswick tells McMurphy that he understands why McMurphy no longer rebels against Ratched. That day, Cheswick's fingers get stuck in the pool's drain and he drowns in what is possibly a suicide.

Sefelt, who has epilepsy, has a seizure on the floor. Fredrickson, also an epileptic, always takes Sefelt's medication. Ratched takes the opportunity to demonstrate the importance of following her advice and not "acting foolish." McMurphy, who has never seen an epileptic seizure, is very disturbed by the whole scenario. Bromden notes that McMurphy is beginning to get a "haggard, puzzled look of pressure" on his face.

Harding's wife comes for a brief visit. Harding mocks her poor grammar, and she says she wishes his limp-wristed friends would stop coming to their house to ask about him. After she leaves, McMurphy angrily erupts when Harding asks for his opinion of her, saying, "I've got worries of my own without getting hooked with yours. So just quit!" The patients are then taken to get chest X rays for TB, and McMurphy learns that Ratched can send anyone she wants for electroshock therapy and even a lobotomy in some cases, despite the fact that both practices are outdated. McMurphy tells the other patients that he knows now why they encouraged his rebellion without informing him about the consequences. He now understands that they submit to her not only because she is able to authorize these treatments, but also because she determines when they can leave the hospital. Harding informs him that, to the contrary, Scanlon is the only Acute aside from McMurphy who is committed. The rest of the Acutes are in the hospital voluntarily and could leave whenever they chose. McMurphy, completely perplexed, asks Billy Bibbit why he chooses to stay when he could be outside driving a convertible and romancing pretty girls. Billy Bibbit begins to cry and shouts that he and the others are not as big, strong, and brave as McMurphy.

McMurphy buys three cartons of cigarettes at the canteen. After the Group Meeting, Ratched announces that she and Doctor Spivey think the patients should be punished for their insubordination against the cleaning schedule a few weeks before. Since they did not apologize or show any remorse, she and Spivey have decided to take away the second game room. Everyone, including the Chronics, turns to see how McMurphy reacts. McMurphy smiles and tips his hat. Ratched thinks that she has regained control, but, after the meeting, McMurphy calmly walks to the glass-enclosed Nurses' Station where she is sitting. He says that he wants some of his cigarettes and punches his hand through the glass. He claims that the glass was so spotless that he forgot it was even there.

ANALYSIS
The staff meeting illustrates the unbelievable extent of Nurse Ratched's power in the hospital, even in the face of disruptions by a clever, sharp-witted patient like McMurphy. After McMurphy learns of her true power—her responsibility for his release and her ability to administer inhumane treatments—no one dares deny her authority even after her hysterical fit. She quickly reconsolidates her power over the staff before they can doubt her. Ratched's actions indicate her clear-thinking, premeditated approach to dealing with McMurphy. She chooses to keep McMurphy on the ward to prevent him from attaining the status of a martyr. Moreover, she realizes that sending him off the ward would be tantamount to declaring defeat. Ratched would rather confront McMurphy directly. She is comforted to know that she has complete control over his future, and that once he realizes it too, he will not dare to disobey her.

Up to this point, McMurphy's rebellions have largely been self-motivated, although they have ended up benefiting others as well. Now the other men are discovering their own individual desires and begin to follow his lead: Cheswick demands that the rationing of cigarettes be ended, and Bromden stops taking his sleeping pill. Bromden's transformation from a pretend deaf-mute into a man who can think for himself results from his observation and admiration of McMurphy. Although Bromden is physically much larger than McMurphy, he sees himself as weak and small, and he marvels at McMurphy's strength. He realizes that McMurphy's power comes from his ability to "be who he is," to maintain his individuality within the Combine's institutions. With this new knowledge, Bromden and the other patients slowly resurrect their suppressed individuality.

Bromden's realization, upon looking out the window, that the hospital is in the countryside symbolizes the broadening of his perceptual abilities under McMurphy's influence. He watches as animals interact with man-made creations. This scene of nature versus machine echoes the situation occurring within the hospital's walls. The geese belong entirely to the wild, undomesticated world. The car represents the oppressive, mechanized modern society. The dog, as a domesticated creature, is situated in between. Bromden notes that the dog and the car are headed for "the same spot of pavement." The implication is that the dog will run into the car and be killed by the overwhelmingly larger machine. This image signifies that when one tries to defy modern society's mechanized, conventional imperatives, one runs the risk of experiencing annihilation rather than victory.

After McMurphy learns that Ratched will determine when he can leave the hospital, he chooses to conform to the hospital's set of norms and rules. McMurphy doesn't yet understand the responsibility that he has assumed by serving as the ward's most effective teacher of resistance. This responsibility becomes apparent when Cheswick dies. McMurphy realizes that by ending his rebellion and conforming to Ratched's ways to save himself, he has become complicit with the destructive Combine.

The knowledge of his own complacency with the Combine strikes McMurphy strongly and influences him to resume his rebellion, although with a new sense of the ramifications of rebellion. He now acts with the full knowledge of his situation and the punishments that Ratched may inflict on him in response to his continued opposition. He now knowingly assumes the role of leader that he naively assumed earlier. Rather than being a selfish action, his resumed rebellion is calculated to benefit the other patients. In addition, McMurphy no longer relies on humorous nettling as his weapon in this rebellion. McMurphy's strength becomes less mental and more corporeal. Breaking the window is his first act of violence—far more serious than his humorous jabs. Moreover, the glass, which is kept so spotless that it is almost invisible, represents the control Nurse Ratched has over the patients; it is so deviously subtle that they sometimes forget it is there. By breaking the glass, McMurphy reminds the other patients that her power over them is always present, while simultaneously suggesting that their knowledge of her power renders that power breakable.

PART III

Summary

After breaking the glass at the Nurses' Station, McMurphy is back to his old troublemaking ways. Even Doctor Spivey begins to assert himself with the nurse. The aides put a piece of cardboard where McMurphy broke the glass, and Ratched continues to sit behind it as if it were transparent—she looks like "a picture turned to the wall." Ratched rejects McMurphy's petition for an Accompanied Pass, which is a permission to spend time outside the ward while attended by another person. McMurphy wants to leave the ward with a prostitute he knows from Portland, Candy Starr. As a result of Ratched's denial, McMurphy shatters the replacement glass pane, claiming he did not know it had been replaced. Bromden notes that the nurse shows signs that her patience is starting to wear down. When the glass is replaced again, Scanlon accidentally smashes it with a basketball, which she then throws away.

Doctor Spivey grants McMurphy's request for a pass to take a fishing trip with nine other patients, accompanied by two of his aunts. Men begin to sign up for the trip, each paying McMurphy ten dollars for the boat rental. Meanwhile, Ratched pins newspaper clippings about rough weather and wrecked boats on the bulletin board. Bromden wants to sign the list, but he is afraid to blow his deaf-and-dumb cover, realizing that he has to "keep acting deaf if [he] wanted to hear at all." He remembers that when he was ten, three people came to his home to talk to his father about buying the tribe's land. When Bromden spoke to them, they acted like he had not said a word. This memory represents the first time in a long time that he has remembered something about his childhood.

Geever, an aide, wakes Bromden and McMurphy in the middle of the night when he scrapes off the wads of gum under Bromden's bed.

He tells McMurphy that he has tried for a long time to find out where Bromden, as an indigent patient, could obtain gum. After he leaves the dorm, McMurphy gives Bromden some Juicy Fruit, and Bromden, before he can think of what he is doing, thanks him. McMurphy tells him that when he was a boy, he took a job picking beans. The adults ignored him, so McMurphy silently listened to their malicious gossip all summer. At the end of the season, he told everyone what the others said in their absence, creating havoc. Bromden replies that he is too little to do something bold like that.

McMurphy offers to make Bromden big again with his special body-building course. He offers to pay Bromden's share of the fishing trip fee if he promises to get strong enough to lift the control panel in the tub room. He tells Bromden that the aunts who will accompany them are in reality two prostitutes. When McMurphy notices Bromden's erection, he states that Bromden is getting bigger already. Right then, McMurphy adds Bromden's name to the list. The next day he persuades George Sorenson, a former fisherman, to take the last slot.

When Candy arrives at the hospital—without Sandy—the men are transfixed by her beauty and femininity. Ratched threatens to cancel the trip because all the patients cannot fit into Candy's car, and they do not have a second driver. In doing so, she discovers that McMurphy lied about the cost of the rental to make a profit off the other patients. She tries to use this information as part of her typical divide-and-conquer strategy, but the other patients do not seem to mind. McMurphy then persuades Doctor Spivey to come with them and drive the second car. When they stop for gas, the attendant tries to take advantage of them. McMurphy gets out of the car and warns him that they are a bunch of crazy, psychopathic murderers. The other patients, seeing that their illness could actually be a source of power for them, lose their nervousness and follow his lead in using their insanity to intimidate the attendant.

Bromden marvels at the changes the Combine has wrought on the Outside—the thousands of mechanized commuters and houses and children. When they get to the docks, the captain of the boat does not allow them to take the trip, because he does not have a signed waiver exonerating him should any accidents occur. Meanwhile, the men on the dock harass Candy, and the patients are ashamed that they are too afraid to stand up for her. To distract the captain of the boat, McMurphy gives him a phone number to call. When the captain goes to call, McMurphy herds the patients onto the boat. They are already out to sea by the time the captain realizes the number belongs to a brothel.

While on the boat, everyone catches large fish and gets drunk. When they return to the dock, the captain is waiting with some policemen. The doctor threatens to inform the authorities that the captain did not provide enough life jackets, so the policemen leave without arresting anyone. After a short fistfight, McMurphy and the captain have a drink together. The men on the dock are friendly with the patients when they see their impressive catches and after they learn that George is a retired fisherman. Billy is infatuated with Candy; when McMurphy notices this, he arranges a date for them at two in the morning two weeks later, on a Saturday night.

Everyone is in high spirits when they return to the ward, but McMurphy seems pale and exhausted. They had taken a detour to pass by an old, run-down house where McMurphy lived as a child. Caught in a tree branch was an old rag, a remnant from the first time he had sex, as a ten-year-old with a girl who was perhaps even younger than he. She gave him her dress to keep as a reminder, and he threw it out the window, where it caught in a tree branch and remained to this day. Bromden remembers seeing his face reflected in the windshield afterward and remarks how it looked "dreadfully tired and strained and *frantic,* like there was not enough time left for something he had to do."

ANALYSIS

McMurphy's rebellion grows more overt as the patients begin to defy Ratched on their own terms. McMurphy still maintains a somewhat humorous edge to his resistance, as his request for an Accompanied Pass demonstrates. By asking to be let out for a day to consort with a prostitute, McMurphy both asserts his sexuality and reminds Ratched that she has failed to emotionally castrate him. By gaining Spivey's approval for the fishing trip, McMurphy demonstrates to Ratched that he does not deem her the highest authority on the ward. Nurse Ratched can only resist his growing influence by trying in vain to frighten the other patients with the newspaper clippings, which fail to suppress them and their new-found individual thinking.

Meanwhile, Bromden begins to attain greater self-knowledge through McMurphy's influence. He remembers the racist government agents coming to his house, and he realizes the origin of his sense of inadequacy and invisibility. Bromden feels himself becoming stronger as he talks to McMurphy and slowly becomes a man in his own eyes. McMurphy's offer of Juicy Fruit to Bromden illustrates the value of good relationships between the patients, and Bromden's decision to speak demonstrates the extent to which goodwill has helped to heal his wounds.

In contrast, Geever's discovery of Bromden's gum is a reminder that the hospital continues to function like a totalitarian state. The patients are still subject to strict supervision and the invasion of their privacy. Once faced with the conniving Geever, Bromden knows that McMurphy will keep his most precious secret: that he is not deaf and dumb. McMurphy's own childhood experience of playing mute shows that the two of them are more similar than they might appear.

McMurphy's own program of therapy for the other patients involves reviving their faith in their sexuality. He notes, jokingly, that Bromden's erection is proof that he is getting bigger already. McMurphy presents the patients with a woman who can reawaken their repressed sex drives; the pretty Candy Starr, unlike Nurse Ratched, exudes sexuality. McMurphy seems to recognize that the patients, Billy in particular, can become individual, powerful men only if they can experience sexual feelings without the sense of shame that Ratched and the rest of the ward seem to inculcate.

During the trip, two unpleasant experiences threaten the therapeutic value of the outing but ultimately lead to the greatest individual development for the patients. First, when the gas station attendant disrespects them, McMurphy rescues them by showing how their stigmatized identity as mental patients can be used to their advantage. Instead of being made to feel afraid, they can now intimidate others by exaggerating their insanity. McMurphy, in effect, teaches them how to cope with the outside world in a different way, to reject the previously unsuccessful approach of conformity. However, the patients still depend heavily on McMurphy to lead them. When they arrive at the docks, they are too timid to answer the insults of the seamen by themselves.

The second experience that initially seems detrimental, but is actually beneficial, occurs when McMurphy tests the patients by refusing to help them once they are out to sea. Like Christ taking his twelve disciples to the sea, he forces them to fend for themselves, and they find, to their surprise, that they do not actually need his help. They begin to see themselves as men, not as feeble mental patients. When they return to the docks, they realize that they not only have proven something to themselves, but they have proven something to the seamen with their impressive catches. In turn, the seamen act politely and respectfully, in remarkable contrast to their earlier rudeness.

Yet, while the mental state of each patient is improving immensely, the strain of responsibility for curing the patients of their society-generated insecurities has clearly begun to wear McMurphy down. McMurphy's exhaustion seems to stem from something other than the trip alone, and Bromden's description of his expression in the car foreshadows McMurphy's eventual submission. Significantly, this expression occurs in conjunction with McMurphy's childhood memory of being sexually dominated by a woman. Despite all of the fervor and individuality that McMurphy conveys, he also has experienced a distortion of his male sexuality due to a woman's dominance. In his increasing strain, we see that the strength which makes McMurphy so well equipped to combat the mechanistic society of Nurse Ratched—his humanity—is also a weakness that may ultimately lead to his total exhaustion.

PART IV

SUMMARY
Nurse Ratched posts the patients' financial statements on the bulletin board to show that everyone's account, except McMurphy's, shows a steady decline in funds. The other patients begin to question the motivations for his actions. When a phone call keeps McMurphy away from a Group Meeting, Ratched insinuates that everything he does is motivated by the desire for personal gain. Later, Harding argues that they have all gotten their money's worth and that McMurphy never hid his con-man ways from them.

McMurphy asks Bromden if he can move the control panel, as a way of testing how big Bromden has grown. Bromden is able to move it half a foot. McMurphy makes a rigged bet with the other patients that someone could lift the control panel, knowing, of course, that Bromden has already lifted it. Bromden lifts it, and McMurphy wins the bet. Bromden, uncomfortable with McMurphy's deceit, refuses to accept the five dollars that McMurphy offers him later. McMurphy asks why all of a sudden everyone acts like he is a traitor, and Bromden tells him it is because he is always winning things.

Ratched orders that everyone who went on the fishing trip be cleansed because of the company they kept. George has a phobia regarding cleanliness and begs the aides not to spray him with their smelly salve. McMurphy and Bromden get into a fistfight with the aides to defend George, so Ratched sends them to Disturbed. The kind Japanese nurse who tends them explains that army nurses have a habit of trying to run the place as if it were an army hospital and are "a little sick themselves." One of the patients wakes Bromden during the night by yelling in his face, "I'm starting to spin, Indian! Look me, look me!" Bromden wonders how McMurphy can sleep, plagued as he must be by "a hundred faces like that," desperate for his attention.

Nurse Ratched tells McMurphy that he can avoid electroshock therapy by admitting he was wrong. He refuses, telling her "those Chinese Commies could have learned a few things from you, lady." He and Bromden are sent for the treatment, but McMurphy does not seem afraid at all. He voluntarily climbs onto the cross-shaped table and wonders aloud if he will get a "crown of thorns." Bromden, however, is afraid and struggles mightily. During the treatment and afterward, Bromden experiences a rush of images and memories from his childhood. When he regains consciousness, he resists the fog and works to clear his head, the first time he has managed to do so after receiving shock therapy. He knows that this time he "had them beat," and he is not subjected to any more treatments. McMurphy, however, receives three more treatments that week. He maintains an unconcerned attitude about it, but Bromden can tell that the treatments are affecting him. Ratched realizes that McMurphy is growing bigger in the eyes of the other men because he is out of sight, so she decides to bring him back from Disturbed.

The other patients know that Ratched will continue to harass McMurphy, so they urge him to escape. McMurphy reminds them that Billy's date with Candy is later that night. That night, McMurphy persuades Turkle to open the window for Candy. She arrives with Sandy in tow, carrying copious amounts of alcohol. Everyone mixes vodka with cough syrup, while Turkle and McMurphy smoke joints. Sefelt has a seizure while with Sandy, and Harding sprinkles pills over them both, declaring that they are "witnessing the end, the absolute, irrevocable, fantastic end." Sometime after four in the morning, Billy and Candy retreat to the Seclusion Room.

As it gets closer to morning, they realize that they are going to have to figure something out before the staff arrives. Harding tells McMurphy that they can tie up Turkle, so it looks like the mess created by their party was all part of McMurphy's escape attempt. Turkle can keep his job, the other patients will not get into trouble, and McMurphy can drive off to Canada or Mexico with Candy and Sandy. McMurphy asks whether any of the rest of them would want to escape with him. Harding replies by saying that he is almost ready to leave on his own, with all "the traditional red tape." He says that the rest of them are "still sick men in lots of ways. But at least there's that: they are sick *men* now. No more rabbits, Mack."

McMurphy and Sandy climb into bed after asking Turkle to wake them up right before the morning staff arrives. Unfortunately, Turkle falls asleep, and the aides discover them in the morning. Bromden surmises that the ensuing repercussions were inevitable, whether or not they followed through with McMurphy's escape. He figures that even if McMurphy had escaped, he would have had to come back and not let the nurse get "the last play."

The next morning all the patients are incredulous about the night's activities. As Ratched turns up more and more incriminating remnants from the party, the patients cannot keep their laughter in, and the nurse looks like she is going to "blow up like a bladder." McMurphy has a chance to escape when Turkle undoes the screen to let Sandy out, but he refuses, despite Harding's warnings of what is to come. When Ratched finds Billy with Candy, he is calm and peaceful. He and Candy both move "like cats full of warm milk." The nurse threatens to tell Billy's mother. Billy regains his stutter and begins to cry, begging her to keep it a secret and blaming Candy, McMurphy, and Harding for the whole thing. She sends him to Spivey's office to wait while she clears things up with the other patients. But Billy ends up committing suicide by cutting his throat.

Nurse Ratched asks McMurphy if he is satisfied with his accomplishments, and then she retreats to the Nurses' Station. Bromden realizes that nobody will be able to stop McMurphy from rebelling, because it is the need of the patients that has been encouraging him all along, "making him wink and grin and laugh and go on with his act long after his humor had been parched dry between two electrodes." Then, McMurphy smashes through the glass door, rips open the front of Ratched's uniform, and tries to strangle her. As he is pried off of the nurse, he gives out a cry "of cornered-animal fear and hate and surrender and defiance."

Several of the Acutes transfer to other wards, and some check themselves out of the hospital altogether. The doctor is asked to resign but refuses. Ratched returns after a week on medical leave with a heavy bandage around her throat, unable to speak. She cannot regain her former power over the ward. Eventually the only patients left on the ward are Bromden, Martini, and Scanlon. McMurphy is given a lobotomy for his attack on Nurse Ratched. When he is returned to the ward after the operation, he is a vegetable. That same night, Bromden suffocates McMurphy with a pillow. He throws the control panel through a window screen and escapes from the hospital, hitching a ride with a trucker.

ANALYSIS

Ratched makes one last feeble attempt to regain control when she uses the same principle she used earlier to ensure the patients' submission to her authority: divide and conquer. She begins to sow the seeds of distrust among the patients by publicizing the financial gain McMurphy has enjoyed since his transfer from the work farm. Harding defends McMurphy, pointing out that McMurphy has more than repaid the patients' financial losses by providing them with the means to resist Ratched's influence.

But it is McMurphy's timing of the rigged bet on the control panel that proves extremely disadvantageous. He fleeces them of their money too soon after Ratched has planted the seeds of doubt in their minds. Bromden is affected most acutely, because he feels that McMurphy has used him to take advantage of the others. Only after McMurphy regains the patients' trust by taking on yet another personal risk for their benefit—defending George against the aides—do Bromden and the others realize McMurphy's true objectives. Even Bromden helps this time, demonstrating the extent to which he has regained his self-confidence.

McMurphy's self-sacrifice for the benefit of the other patients begins to surface after he defends George, and also when he undergoes the electroshock treatments. McMurphy is belted to a cross-shaped table, an obvious allusion to a crucifix. This Christ imagery suggests an impending martyrdom on the part of McMurphy, and he even compares himself to Christ when he asks whether he gets to wear a crown of thorns. Of course, a martyr ultimately must sacrifice himself to save others. This proves true, since although Bromden feels strong enough to withstand the effects of the electroshock, McMurphy weakens under the repeated treatments. Bromden finally begins to feel that his victory over the hospital is complete. He is no longer ruled by his fears or his past, thanks to the help of his unlikely savior, McMurphy.

After Nurse Ratched provokes Billy, leading to his suicide, McMurphy truly does become a Christ figure for the patients. Under the invisible but heavy pressure of the other patients' expectations, McMurphy makes the ultimate sacrifice to ensure that Ratched cannot use Billy's death to undo everything they have gained. By attacking Ratched and ripping her uniform, he permanently breaks her power but also forfeits his own life. Though Ratched tries to give McMurphy a fate worse than death by having him lobotomized, Bromden dignifies McMurphy by killing him, assuring that McMurphy will always be a symbol of resistance instead of a lingering cautionary tale for future patients on Ratched's ward.

IMPORTANT QUOTATIONS EXPLAINED

1. I been silent so long now it's gonna roar out of me like
    floodwaters and you think the guy telling this is
    ranting and raving my *God*; you think this is too
    horrible to have really happened, this is too awful to
    be the truth! But, please. It's still hard for me to have a
    clear mind thinking on it. But it's the truth even if it
    didn't happen.

We are given this brainteaser from Chief Bromden in Part 1. The
reader has already gotten a glimpse of Bromden's paranoia, from
the novel's opening lines, as well as a sense that he is not seeing
things from an everyday perspective. For example, Bromden
describes Nurse Ratched transforming into a huge machine, and he
has to be sedated when the aides try to shave him and he starts
screaming "Air Raid." Up until this point he has not addressed the
reader directly; it is as though we are overhearing his private
thoughts. But in this passage he asserts himself as not only the narrator but the author of the story. We learn here that he has an important story to tell, even though it is going to be difficult. The ugly and
violent images that he has already shown us, he warns us, are just a
taste of what is to come.

The last line of the quote is Bromden's request that the reader
keep an open mind. His hallucinations provide metaphorical insight
into the hidden realities of the hospital and should not be over-
looked simply because they did not actually happen. Although over
the course of the novel Bromden regains his sanity, he still witnesses
many of the events while in a semi-catatonic, hallucinatory state; we
have to trust in the truth of his sharp perceptions, no matter what
form they take.

2. The flock gets sight of a spot of blood on some
    chicken and they all go to *peckin'* at it, see, till they rip
    the chicken to shreds, blood and bones and feathers.
    But usually a couple of the *flock* gets spotted in the
    fracas, then it's their turn. And a few more gets spots
    and gets pecked to death, and more and more. Oh, a
    peckin' party can wipe out the whole flock in a matter
    of a few hours, buddy, I seen it. A mighty awesome
    sight. The only way to prevent it—with chickens—is
    to clip blinders on them. So's they can't see.

McMurphy gives this explanation to Harding and the other patients
in Part I after his first Group Meeting. The entire group had been
tearing into Harding, adhering to Doctor Spivey's theory of the
"Therapeutic Community," where the patients are encouraged to
bring "old sins out into the open." Afterward, McMurphy tells the
other patients that they were like "a bunch of chickens at a peckin'
party," attacking the weakest one with such blind fury that they all
put themselves in danger.

McMurphy is immediately shocked by the behavior of the
patients and staff. It is clear to him that Ratched maintains her
power through such strategies as divide and conquer. He points out
that she "pecks the first peck," or points out the first weakness, and
then just sits back and watches as the patients start to attack each
other. He does not understand why the patients fall for this strategy,
especially since they might be next in line as the object of ridicule.
The patients do seem to have blinders on; they are so blinded by
their own shame that they are unable to see Ratched's true nature
and the way she manipulates and controls them so effortlessly.

3.   So you see my friend, it is somewhat as you stated:
     man has but *one* truly effective weapon against the
     juggernaut of modern matriarchy, but it certainly is
     not laughter. One weapon, and with every passing
     year in this hip, motivationally researched society,
     more and more people are discovering how to render
     that weapon useless and conquer those who have
     hitherto been conquerors. . . .

This passage occurs later in the same discussion that followed
McMurphy's first Group Meeting in Part 1. Here, Kesey begins to
develop his misogynistic theory about modern society. Harding is
talking to McMurphy, explaining that men's one weapon against
women is the penis, and that if men are unable to use rape effec-
tively, they have no chance to regain power in society. Kesey
believes that women have learned this, and they now know how to
render men's one weapon useless—in other words, they are all ball-
cutters. Where rape is the male means to power, castration is the
female way to domination.

   These crude ideas are given substance throughout the novel.
Kesey uses McMurphy's fearless sexuality as a sign that he is sane.
McMurphy goads Ratched sexually by wearing just a towel, pinch-
ing her rear, remarking on her breasts, and eventually tearing her
shirt open. Most of the male patients have stories about damaging
relationships with women, such as Bromden's mother, Billy Bibbit's
mother and onetime girlfriend, and Harding's wife. When McMurphy notices Bromden's erection, a sign that he is "getting bigger
already," it signifies that Bromden is becoming more powerful and
saner. Similarly, through sex with Candy, Billy briefly regains his
confidence and his manhood, until Ratched takes it away and he
commits suicide. Moreover, Ratched and the hospital supervisor,
also a woman, wield all the power in the hospital: "We are victims
of a matriarchy here," says Harding.

4.   Except the sun, on these three strangers, is all of a
     sudden way the hell brighter than usual and I can see
     the . . . *seams* where they're put together. And, almost,
     see the apparatus inside them take the words I just
     said and try to fit the words in here and there, this
     place and that, and when they find the words don't
     have any place ready-made where they'll fit, the
     machinery disposes of the words like they weren't
     even spoken.

In this passage from the beginning of Part III, Bromden, who has
been gaining self-awareness since McMurphy's arrival on the ward,
remembers a scarring experience he had as a ten-year-old. Three
government officials came to speak to his father, Chief Tee Ah Millatoona, about buying the tribe's land to build a hydroelectric dam.
When Bromden tried to speak to them, he noticed that "[n]ot a one
of the three acts like they heard a thing [he] said." He begins to see
the world differently, believing that he can see the seams on people,
as though they were inhuman or machine-like.

   For Kesey, the drones who do the dirty work of an oppressive
society are basically machines. The government officials who visited
Bromden's father were planning to make a profit by destroying
nature, represented by the tribe's ancient connection to the land, the
river, and the fish, and replacing it with destructive technology. The
brightness of the sun sheds light on the dark fact these officials
taught Bromden: that people who do not have "any place ready-
made where they'll fit" are ignored and disposed of. At first the
"machinery" disposes of Bromden's words; then, over time, it seems
to ignore his entire being.

5. While McMurphy laughs. Rocking farther and farther backward against the cabin top, spreading his laugh out across the water—laughing at the girl, the guys, at George, at me sucking my bleeding thumb, at the captain back at the pier and the bicycle rider and the service-station guys and the five thousand houses and the Big Nurse and all of it. Because he knows you have to laugh at the things that hurt you just to keep yourself in balance, just to keep the world from running you plumb crazy.

While on the fishing expedition, the patients are able to laugh freely and feel like whole humans again. As usual, this happens with McMurphy's guidance—he is an example for all the patients to follow. Here, Bromden shows how McMurphy's booming laughter in the face of chaos, which could be seen as the mark of a psychopath, is the one thing that keeps McMurphy sane.

Bromden implies that it is the pressures of society—the captain, the five thousand houses, the Big Nurse, "the things that hurt you"—that drive people insane. To maintain sanity in such an oppressive and cruel world, people cannot allow these external forces to exert too much power. When a person succumbs to seeing and experiencing all the sadness and suffering of humanity, as Bromden has done for ten years, it naturally makes him or her unable, or unwilling, to cope with reality—in other words, it can make that person "plumb crazy."

QUOTATIONS

Key Facts

FULL TITLE
One Flew Over the Cuckoo's Nest

AUTHOR
Ken Kesey

TYPE OF WORK
Novel

GENRE
Allegorical novel; counterculture novel; protest novel

LANGUAGE
English

TIME AND PLACE WRITTEN
The late 1950s; at Stanford University in California while Kesey was enrolled in the creative writing program, working as an orderly in a psychiatric ward, and participating in experimental LSD trials

DATE OF FIRST PUBLICATION
1962

PUBLISHER
Viking Press

NARRATOR
Chief Bromden, also known as Chief Broom, who tells the story after he has escaped from the hospital

POINT OF VIEW
Chief Bromden narrates in the first person. He tells the story as it appears to him, though his objectivity is somewhat compromised by the fact that he suffers from paranoia and hallucinations. His unusual state of mind provides metaphorical insight into the insidious reality of the hospital as well as society in general. Because he pretends to be deaf and dumb, he is privy to secret staff information that is kept from other patients, which makes him a more reliable narrator than any other patient would be.

TONE

The novel's tone is critical and allegorical; the hospital is presented as a metaphor for the oppressive society of the late 1950s. The novel praises the expression of sexuality as the ultimate goal and denounces repression as based on fear and hate. Bromden's psychedelic and slightly paranoid worldview may be commensurate with Kesey's, and McMurphy's use of mischief and humor to undermine authority also seems to echo the author's attitudes.

TENSE

Present

SETTING (TIME)

1950s

SETTING (PLACE)

A mental hospital in Oregon

PROTAGONIST

Randle P. McMurphy

MAJOR CONFLICT

The patients in the mental ward are cowed and repressed by the emasculating Nurse Ratched, who represents the oppressive force of modern society. McMurphy tries to lead them to rebel against her authority by asserting their individuality and sexuality, while Nurse Ratched attempts to discredit McMurphy and shame the patients back into docility.

RISING ACTION

The World Series rebellion; McMurphy's encounter with the lifeguard; McMurphy discovering what being committed means; Cheswick's death

CLIMAX

McMurphy reasserts himself against Nurse Ratched at the end of Part II by smashing the glass window in the Nurses' Station, signaling that his rebellion is no longer lighthearted or selfish but committed and violent. McMurphy takes on the responsibility for rehabilitating the other patients.

FALLING ACTION

McMurphy's decision to return Bromden to his former strength; the fishing trip and visit to McMurphy's childhood house, where Bromden sees his panic and fatigue; McMurphy and Bromden's fight with the aides; the electroshock therapy; the ward party and Billy's suicide; McMurphy's violent attack on Nurse Ratched; the lobotomy

THEMES

Women as castrators; society's destruction of natural impulses; the importance of expressing sexuality; false diagnoses of insanity

MOTIFS

Invisibility; the power of laughter; real versus imagined size

SYMBOLS

The fog machine; McMurphy's boxer shorts; the electroshock therapy table

FORESHADOWING

The story of Maxwell Taber; the electroshock therapy table shaped like a cross; the deaths of Rawler, Cheswick, and Billy; Bromden's dreams and hallucinations

Study Questions & Essay Topics

Study Questions

1. *How does Kesey make the reader question the accepted definitions of "sane," "insane," "sick," and "healthy"?*

Bromden sees modern society as an oppressive, mechanizing force, and he views the hospital as a repair shop for the people who do not fit into their roles as cogs in the machine. His way of interpreting the world emphasizes the social pressure to conform. Those who do not conform to the rules and conventions of society are considered defective products of the "schools, churches, and neighborhoods." Such people are labeled mentally ill and sent for treatment. The hospital is normally defined as the place where the ill go to be cured. However, in the cases of Ellis, Ruckly, and Taber, the cure—being in the psychiatric hospital—is obviously worse than the disease. Ellis and Ruckly are considered "failures," but Taber is considered a success. However, it is hard to tell the difference between the cured and sick patients. Taber, the cured patient, functions like a robot incapable of independent thought after he leaves the hospital; as such, he fits perfectly into society.

2.   *Why is the fishing trip therapeutic for the patients?*

When the gas station attendant tries to intimidate the patients and the doctor into accepting services they do not want, McMurphy comes to their rescue by showing them how their stigmatized identity as mental patients can be used to their advantage. Instead of being made to feel afraid, they can inspire fear in others by exaggerating their insanity. McMurphy tries to teach the other patients another way to cope with the outside world, without using an approach of total conformity. However, when they arrive at the docks, they are too timid to answer the insults of the seamen without the support of McMurphy. Once they are out to sea, McMurphy refuses to step in and aid the patients. He leaves them to manage things for themselves, and, to their surprise, they find they do not actually need his help. They begin to see themselves as men, not as feeble mental patients. When the patients return to the docks, they realize that they have proven something to themselves and to the outside world, and the seamen are impressed by their large catches from the sea.

3.   *How does McMurphy become a Christ figure?*

Several images contribute to the perception of McMurphy as a Christ figure. He is baptized with a shower upon entering the ward. He takes the patients on a fishing trip, like Jesus and his twelve disciples, to test and strengthen their faith in him and his rehabilitation methods. When McMurphy is taken to get electroshock treatment, he lies down voluntarily on the cross-shaped table and asks whether he will get his "crown of thorns." Under the weighty pressure of the other patients' expectations, McMurphy makes the ultimate sacrifice to ensure that Ratched cannot use Billy's death to undo everything they have gained. He sacrifices his own hopes of personal salvation when he violently attacks her. McMurphy rips her uniform to reveal her femininity, the evidence that she is not an all-powerful machine but a flesh-and-blood person. His deed succeeds in destroying Ratched's power. Although he himself dies as a result, his sacrifice becomes an inspiration to the other patients.

SUGGESTED ESSAY TOPICS

1. How is Nurse Ratched's ward like a totalitarian society?

2. *One Flew Over the Cuckoo's Nest* has been criticized for its treatment of race and gender. Why do you think this is the case?

3. McMurphy, Colonel Matterson, and Bromden are war veterans. Nurse Ratched is a former army nurse who tries to run her ward as if it were an army hospital. How might the advent of modern warfare serve as a metaphor for the sickness that Kesey perceives in modern society?

4. Why is Bromden the narrator of *One Flew Over the Cuckoo's Nest* instead of McMurphy? Who is the real protagonist of the novel? How does the use of Bromden as the narrator tie into the biblical allusions in the novel?

REVIEW & RESOURCES

QUIZ

1. What physical feature does Nurse Ratched try to conceal?

   A. Her long legs
   B. Her blonde hair
   C. Her large breasts
   D. Her birthmark

2. Why did Nurse Ratched hire the three black aides?

   A. For their strength
   B. For their intelligence
   C. For their stubbornness
   D. For their hatred

3. What animals does McMurphy compare the patients to?

   A. Wolves
   B. Chickens
   C. Rabbits
   D. Pigs

4. What animals does Harding compare the patients to?

   A. Wolves
   B. Chickens
   C. Rabbits
   D. Pigs

5. What pattern covers McMurphy's boxer shorts?

   A. White whales
   B. Hearts
   C. Rabbits
   D. Kisses

6.   Which character is a closeted homosexual?

    A.   Nurse Ratched
    B.   Billy Bibbit
    C.   Dale Harding
    D.   Chief Bromden

7.   Which patient has been on the ward the longest?

    A.   Pete Bancini
    B.   Colonel Matterson
    C.   Chief Bromden
    D.   Maxwell Taber

8.   How does Rawler, a patient on Disturbed, commit suicide?

    A.   He hangs himself
    B.   He drowns
    C.   He cuts off his testicles
    D.   He slits his throat

9.   Which of the following symbolizes Bromden's insanity?

    A.   The flock of geese
    B.   The loud music
    C.   The monopoly board
    D.   The fog machine

10.   What is the reward for snitching on a fellow patient?

    A.   Sleeping late
    B.   An extra pack of cigarettes
    C.   An Accompanied Pass
    D.   Skipping the Group Meeting

11.   What is McMurphy's first complaint to Nurse Ratched?

    A.   That the bathrooms are dirty
    B.   That the music is played too loudly
    C.   That he has no privacy
    D.   That he cannot smoke the cigarettes he bought

REVIEW & RESOURCES

12. What ailment do Sefelt and Fredrickson suffer from?

    A.   Diabetes
    B.   Multiple sclerosis
    C.   Jaundice
    D.   Epilepsy

13. Why does Doctor Spivey drive the patients and accompany them on the fishing trip?

    A.   It is hospital policy to have a member of the staff accompany, and Ratched refuses to go
    B.   The original driver, Sandy, does not show up
    C.   Spivey is a former fisherman who insists he can show McMurphy how it is done
    D.   He loses a bet to McMurphy and has no choice

14. Which character, a former seaman, captains the fishing boat?

    A.   Colonel Matterson
    B.   George Sorensen
    C.   Doctor Spivey
    D.   Dale Harding

15. What is McMurphy's excuse for breaking through the glass of the Nurses' Station?

    A.   The glass was so clean he did not see it
    B.   Voices in his head told him to
    C.   The patients bet him he would not do it
    D.   He tripped

16. What important information does the lifeguard give McMurphy?

    A.   That Doctor Spivey is addicted to opiates
    B.   That he was once in the NFL
    C.   That committed patients can leave only at the staff's discretion
    D.   That Bromden is crazy

17. Which of Nurse Ratched's patients dies in the novel?

    A. Billy Bibbit
    B. Charles Cheswick
    C. Randle McMurphy
    D. All of the above

18. What punishment do McMurphy and Bromden receive for fighting with the aides?

    A. They have to clean the latrines
    B. They have to give up card games in the tub room
    C. They are given electroshock therapy
    D. They are given lobotomies

19. What does McMurphy do to Nurse Ratched after Billy commits suicide?

    A. He punches her in the face
    B. He rips open her shirt and strangles her
    C. He rips off her clothes and rapes her
    D. He calls her vulgar names to her face

20. Why doesn't Harding want to escape with McMurphy?

    A. He wants to leave via the correct procedures, to prove that he can
    B. He is afraid of the outside and prefers the hospital
    C. He is too drunk and he passes out
    D. He promised his wife that he would stay another year

21. How does Chief Bromden leave the hospital?

    A. He leaves with Candy and Sandy through the window
    B. He checks himself out
    C. He makes Doctor Spivey drive him away
    D. He breaks through a window and runs away

REVIEW & RESOURCES

22. How does Charles Cheswick die?

    A. He falls off the boat during the fishing trip and drowns
    B. He drowns in the hospital swimming pool
    C. He receives too many electroshock treatments
    D. He has an epileptic seizure

23. What might the white whales on McMurphy's boxers symbolize?

    A. An obsessive search for evil
    B. The power of nature
    C. God
    D. All of the above

24. Which event symbolizes that Bromden is regaining his sense of self?

    A. He watches the dog outside his window
    B. He smashes the glass of the Nurse's Station
    C. He helps McMurphy win a bet by lifting the control panel
    D. He sweeps the floor during a Group Meeting

25. Who eventually kills McMurphy?

    A. Nurse Ratched
    B. McMurphy commits suicide
    C. Doctor Spivey
    D. Bromden

SUGGESTIONS FOR FURTHER READING

KAPPEL, LAWRENCE, ed. *Readings on* ONE FLEW OVER THE CUCKOO'S NEST. San Diego: Greenhaven Press, 2000.

LEEDS, BARRY H. *Ken Kesey.* New York: F. Ungar Publishing Co., 1981.

PERRY, PAUL. *On the Bus: The Complete Guide to the Legendary Trip of Ken Kesey and the Merry Pranksters and the Birth of the Counterculture.* New York: Thunder's Mouth Press, 1996.

PORTER, M. GILBERT. ONE FLEW OVER THE CUCKOO'S NEST: *Rising to Heroism.* Boston: Twayne, 1989.

SAFER, ELAINE B. *The Contemporary American Comic Epic: The Novels of Barth, Pynchon, Gaddis, and Kesey.* Detroit: Wayne State University Press, 1988.

SEARLES, GEORGE J., ed. *A Casebook on Ken Kesey's One Flew Over the Cuckoo's Nest.* Albuquerque: University of New Mexico Press, 1992.

WHITMER, PETER O. *Aquarius Revisited: Seven Who Created the Sixties Counterculture that Changed America.* New York: Macmillan, 1987.

REVIEW & RESOURCES

SparkNotes™ Literature Guides

1984
The Adventures of
  Huckleberry Finn
The Adventures of Tom
  Sawyer
The Aeneid
All Quiet on the
  Western Front
And Then There Were
  None
Angela's Ashes
Animal Farm
Anna Karenina
Anne of Green Gables
Anthem
Antony and Cleopatra
Aristotle's Ethics
As I Lay Dying
As You Like It
Atlas Shrugged
The Awakening
The Autobiography of
  Malcolm X
The Bean Trees
The Bell Jar
Beloved
Beowulf
Billy Budd
Black Boy
Bless Me, Ultima
The Bluest Eye
Brave New World
The Brothers
  Karamazov
The Call of the Wild
Candide
The Canterbury Tales
Catch-22
The Catcher in the Rye
The Chocolate War
The Chosen
Cold Mountain
Cold Sassy Tree
The Color Purple
The Count of Monte
  Cristo
Crime and Punishment
The Crucible
Cry, the Beloved
  Country
Cyrano de Bergerac
David Copperfield

Death of a Salesman
The Death of Socrates
The Diary of a Young
  Girl
A Doll's House
Don Quixote
Dr. Faustus
Dr. Jekyll and Mr. Hyde
Dracula
Dune
East of Eden
Edith Hamilton's
  Mythology
Emma
Ethan Frome
Fahrenheit 451
Fallen Angels
A Farewell to Arms
Farewell to Manzanar
Flowers for Algernon
For Whom the Bell
  Tolls
The Fountainhead
Frankenstein
The Giver
The Glass Menagerie
Gone With the Wind
The Good Earth
The Grapes of Wrath
Great Expectations
The Great Gatsby
Greek Classics
Grendel
Gulliver's Travels
Hamlet
The Handmaid's Tale
Hard Times
Harry Potter and the
  Sorcerer's Stone
Heart of Darkness
Henry IV, Part I
Henry V
Hiroshima
The Hobbit
The House of Seven
  Gables
I Know Why the Caged
  Bird Sings
The Iliad
Inferno
Inherit the Wind
Invisible Man

Jane Eyre
Johnny Tremain
The Joy Luck Club
Julius Caesar
The Jungle
The Killer Angels
King Lear
The Last of the
  Mohicans
Les Miserables
A Lesson Before Dying
The Little Prince
Little Women
Lord of the Flies
The Lord of the Rings
Macbeth
Madame Bovary
A Man for All Seasons
The Mayor of
  Casterbridge
The Merchant of Venice
A Midsummer Night's
  Dream
Moby Dick
Much Ado About
  Nothing
My Antonia
Narrative of the Life of
  Frederick Douglass
Native Son
The New Testament
Night
Notes from
  Underground
The Odyssey
The Oedipus Plays
Of Mice and Men
The Old Man and the
  Sea
The Old Testament
Oliver Twist
The Once and Future
  King
One Day in the Life of
  Ivan Denisovich
One Flew Over the
  Cuckoo's Nest
One Hundred Years of
  Solitude
Othello
Our Town
The Outsiders

Paradise Lost
A Passage to India
The Pearl
The Picture of Dorian
  Gray
Poe's Short Stories
A Portrait of the Artist
  as a Young Man
Pride and Prejudice
The Prince
A Raisin in the Sun
The Red Badge of
  Courage
The Republic
Richard III
Robinson Crusoe
Romeo and Juliet
The Scarlet Letter
A Separate Peace
Silas Marner
Sir Gawain and the
  Green Knight
Slaughterhouse-Five
Snow Falling on Cedars
Song of Solomon
The Sound and the Fury
Steppenwolf
The Stranger
Streetcar Named
  Desire
The Sun Also Rises
A Tale of Two Cities
The Taming of the
  Shrew
The Tempest
Tess of the d'Ubervilles
Their Eyes Were
  Watching God
Things Fall Apart
The Things They
  Carried
To Kill a Mockingbird
To the Lighthouse
Treasure Island
Twelfth Night
Ulysses
Uncle Tom's Cabin
Walden
War and Peace
Wuthering Heights
A Yellow Raft in Blue
  Water